SCHOLASTIC

25 Complex Text Passages to Meet the Common Core

Literature and Informational Texts

Grade 2

by Martin Lee and Marcia Miller

NEW YORK ● TORONTO ● LONDON ● AUCKLAND ● SYDNEY
MEXICO CITY ● NEW DELHI ● HONG KONG ● BUENOS AIRES

Teaching *Resources*

Scholastic Inc. grants teachers permission to photocopy the reproducible pages from this book for classroom use. No other part of this publication may be reproduced in whole or in part, or stored in a retrieval system, or transmitted in any form or by any means, electronic, mechanical, photocopying, recording, or otherwise, without written permission of the publisher. For information regarding permission, write to Scholastic Inc., 557 Broadway, New York, NY 10012.

Cover design: Scott Davis
Interior design: Kathy Massaro

Interior illustrations: Teresa Anderko, Delana Bettoli, Mike Gordon, James Graham Hale, Aleksey and Olga Ivanov, Mike Moran, and Bari Weissman © 2014 by Scholastic Inc.

Image credits: page 32 © Janet Lindenmuth/flickr; page 56 © tassel78/Shutterstock, Inc.; page 58 © Thomas Kristich; page 66 © Clenpies Design/Shutterstock, Inc.; page 68 (left) © Shapiso/Shutterstock, Inc.; page 68 (right) © Iancu Cristian/Shutterstock, Inc.; page 70 (top) © Ola Lundqvist/Shutterstock, Inc.; page 70 (center) © Dirk Ercken/Shutterstock, Inc.; page 70 (bottom) © Jeff Banke/Shutterstock, Inc.; page 72 © rafer/Big Stock Photo.

ISBN: 978-0-545-57708-3

2 3 4 5 6 7 8 9 10   40   21 20 19 18 17 16 15 14

Contents

" To build a foundation for college and career readiness, students must read widely and deeply from among a broad range of high-quality, increasingly challenging literary and informational texts. Through extensive reading of stories, dramas, poems, and myths from diverse cultures and different time periods, students gain literary and cultural knowledge as well as familiarity with various text structures and elements. By reading texts in history/social studies, science, and other disciplines, students build a foundation of knowledge in these fields that will also give them the background to be better readers in all content areas. Students can only gain this foundation when the curriculum is intentionally and coherently structured to develop rich content knowledge within and across grades. Students also acquire the habits of reading independently and closely, which are essential to their future success. "

—COMMON CORE STATE STANDARDS FOR ENGLISH LANGUAGE ARTS, JUNE 2010

25 Complex Text Passages to Meet the Common Core: Literature and Informational Texts—Grade 2 includes complex reading passages with companion comprehension question pages for teaching the two types of texts—Literature and Informational—covered in the Common Core State Standards (CCSS) for English Language Arts. The passages and lessons in this book address the rigorous expectations put forth by the CCSS "that students read increasingly complex texts through the grades." This book embraces nine of the ten CCSS College and Career Readiness Anchor Standards for Reading that inform solid instruction for literary and informational texts.

Anchor Standards for Reading

Key Ideas and Details

1. Read closely to determine what the text says explicitly and make logical inferences from it; cite specific textual evidence when writing or speaking to support conclusions drawn from the text.

2. Determine central ideas or themes of a text; summarize key supporting details and ideas.

3. Analyze how and why individuals, events, and ideas develop and interact throughout a text.

Craft and Structure

4. Interpret words and phrases as they are used in a text, including determining technical, connotative, and figurative meanings, and analyze how specific word choices shape meaning or tone.

5. Analyze the structure of texts, including how specific sentences, paragraphs, and larger portions of text relate to each other and the whole.

6. Assess how point of view or purpose shapes the content and style of a text.

Integration of Knowledge and Ideas

7. Integrate and evaluate content presented in diverse media and formats, including visually and quantitatively, as well as in words.

8. Delineate and evaluate the argument and specific claims in a text, including the validity of the reasoning as well as the relevance and sufficiency of the evidence.

Range of Reading and Level of Text Complexity

10. Read and comprehend complex literary and informational texts independently and proficiently.

The materials in this book also address the Foundational Standards for Reading, including skills in phonics, word recognition, and fluency; as well as Language Standards, such as the conventions of standard English, knowledge of language, and vocabulary acquisition and use. In addition, students build writing skills as they answer questions about the passages, demonstrating their ability to convey ideas coherently, clearly, and with support from the text. On page 12, you'll find a correlation chart that details how the 25 passages meet specific reading and language standards. This information can also be found with the teaching notes for each passage on pages 13–25.

About Text Complexity

The CCSS recommend that students tackle increasingly complex texts to develop and hone their skills and knowledge. Many factors contribute to the complexity of any text.

Text complexity is more intricate than a readability score alone reveals. Most formulas examine sentence length and structure and the number of difficult words. Each formula gives different weight to different factors. Other aspects of text complexity include coherence, organization, motivation, and any prior knowledge readers may bring.

A complex text can be relatively easy to decode, but if it examines complex issues or uses figurative language, the overall text complexity rises. By contrast, a text that uses unfamiliar words may be less daunting if readers can apply word-study skills and context clues effectively to determine meaning.

This triangular model used by the CCSS shows three distinct yet interrelated factors that contribute to text complexity.

CCSS Model of Text Complexity

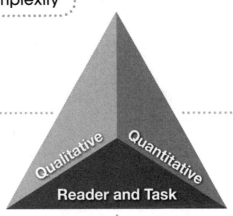

Qualitative measures consider the complexity of meaning or purpose, structure, language conventionality, and overall clarity.

Quantitative measures complexity in terms of word length and frequency, sentence length, and text cohesion. Lexile® algorithms rank this type of complexity on a numerical scale.

Reader and Task considerations refer to such variables as a student's motivation, knowledge, and experience brought to the text, and the purpose, complexity, and types of questions posed.

About the Passages

The 25 reproducible, one-page passages included in this book are divided into two categories. The first 9 passages represent literature (fiction) and are followed by 16 informational texts (nonfiction). Each grouping presents a variety of genres and forms, organizational structures, purposes, tones, and tasks. Consult the table of contents (page 3) to see the scope of genres, forms, and types of content-area texts. The passages within each category are arranged in order of Lexile score (the quantitative measure), from lowest to highest, and fall within the Lexile score ranges recommended for second graders. The Lexile scores for grade 2, revised to reflect the more rigorous demands of the CCSS, range from 420 to 650. For more about determinations of complexity levels, see page 5 and pages 8–9.

Each passage appears on its own page beginning with the title, the genre or form of the passage, and an opening question to give students a focus to keep in mind as they read. Some passages also include visual elements, such as photographs, drawings, illustrations, or tables, as well as typical text elements, such as italics, boldface type, bulleted or numbered lists, subheadings, or sidebars.

The line numbers that appear to the left of each passage will help you and your students readily locate a specific line of text. For example, students might say, "I'm not sure how to pronounce the name here in line 4." They might also include line numbers to identify text evidence when they answer questions about the piece. For example: "The author says in lines 11–13 that…"

The passages are stand-alone texts and can be used in any order you choose. Feel free to assign passages to individuals, small groups, or the entire class, as best suits your teaching style. However, it's a good idea to preview each passage before you assign it, to ensure that your students have the skills needed to complete it successfully. (See page 10 for a close-reading routine to model for students.)

About the After-Reading Question Pages

The Common Core standards suggest that assessment should involve "text-dependent questions." Questions constructed to meet this demand guide students to cite evidence from the text. They fall into three broad categories: 1) Key Ideas and Details, 2) Craft and Structure, and 3) Integration of Knowledge and Ideas. According to the standards, responses should include claims supported by the text, connections to informational or literary elements found within the text explicitly or by logical implication, and age-appropriate analyses of themes or topics.

Following each passage is a reproducible page with four text-dependent comprehension questions for students to answer after reading. Two are multiple-choice questions that call for a single response and a brief text-based explanation to justify that choice. The other questions are open response items. These address a range of comprehension strategies and skills. Students can revisit the passage to find the evidence they need to answer each question. All questions share the goal of ensuring that students engage in close reading of the text, grasp its key ideas, and provide text-based evidence in their answers. In addition, the questions are formatted to reflect the types of questions that will be asked on standardized tests. The questions generally proceed from easier to more complex:

❋ The **least challenging** questions call for basic understanding and recall of details. They involve referencing the text verbatim or paraphrasing it. This kind of question might also ask students to identify a supporting detail an author did or did not include when making a persuasive argument.

❋ The **mid-level** questions call upon students to use mental processes beyond basic recall. To answer these questions, students may need to use context clues to unlock the meaning of unfamiliar words and phrases (including figurative language), classify or compare information, make inferences, distinguish facts from opinions, or make predictions. Such a question might also ask students to summarize the main idea(s) of a passage.

❋ The **deeper** questions focus on understanding that goes beyond the text. Students may need to recognize the author's tone and purpose, make inferences about the entire passage, or use logic to make predictions. This kind of question might even call upon students to determine why an author began or ended the passage as he or she did.

You may find it useful to have students reference line numbers from the passage for efficiency and clarity when they formulate answers. They can also refer to the line numbers during class discussions. Provide additional paper so students have ample space to write complete and thorough answers.

An answer key (pages 76–79) includes sample answers based on textual evidence and specific line numbers from the passage that support the answers. You might want to review answers with the whole class. This approach provides opportunities for discussion, comparison, extension, reinforcement, and correlation to other skills and lessons in your current plans. Your observations can direct the kinds of review and reinforcement you may want to add to subsequent lessons.

About the Teaching Notes

Each passage in this book is supported by a set of teaching notes found on pages 13–25.

In the left column, you will see the following features for each set of teaching notes.

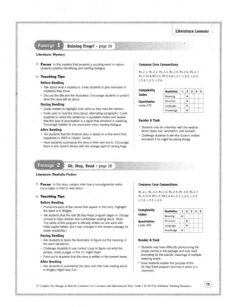

❋ Grouping (**Literature** or **Informational Text**) and the genre or form of the piece.

❋ **Focus** statement describing the essential purpose of the passage, its main features, areas of emphasis, and what students will gain by reading it.

❋ **Teaching Tips** to help you motivate, support, and guide students before, during, and after reading. These easy-to-use suggestions are by no means exhaustive, and you may choose to add or substitute your own ideas or strategies.

- **Before Reading** tips include ways to introduce a passage, explain a genre, present a topic, discuss a format, introduce key vocabulary, or put a theme in context. A tip may suggest how to engage prior knowledge, connect with similar materials in other curriculum areas, or build motivation.

- **During Reading** tips offer possible procedures to help students work through the text, ideas for highlighting key words or concepts, suggestions for graphic organizers, and so on.

- **After Reading** tips provide follow-up questions, discussion topics, extension activities, further readings, or writing assignments linked to the text.

In the right column, are the essential CCSS connections for the passage sorted according to the specific sections of the document: **RL** (Reading Standards for Literature) or **RI** (Reading Standards for Informational Text), **RF** (Reading Standards: Foundational Skills), and **L** (Language Standards). The CCSS chart on page 12 provides the correlations for the entire book at a glance and a URL for the CCSS website where you can find the specific wording of each skill.

Under the essential CCSS connections, you will find a **Complexity Index**, which offers analytical information about the passage based on the three aspects of text complexity, briefly summarized on the next page.

❋ **Quantitative** value, represented by a Lexile score.

❋ **Qualitative** rating, which appears in a matrix that presents four aspects of this measure:

- **Meaning** for literary texts (single level of meaning ↔ multiple levels of meaning) or **Purpose** for informational texts (explicitly stated purpose ↔ implicit purpose)

- **Structure** (simple ↔ complex organization; simple ↔ complex graphics)

- **Language** (literal ↔ figurative; clear ↔ ambiguous; familiar ↔ unusual; conversational ↔ formal)

- **Knowledge** (life experience; content expectations; cultural or literary background needed)

Each of the above aspects are ranked from 1 to 5, briefly summarized, as follows:

1	2	3	4	5
Simple, clear text; accessible language, ideas, and/or structure	Mostly linear with explicit meaning/purpose; clear structure; moderate vocabulary; assumes some knowledge	May have more than one meaning/purpose; some figurative language; more demanding structure, syntax, language, and/or vocabulary; assumes some knowledge	Multiple meanings/purposes possible; more sophisticated syntax, structure, language, and/or vocabulary; assumes much knowledge	May require inference and/or synthesis; complex structure, syntax, language, and/or vocabulary; assumes extensive knowledge

❋ **Reader and Task** considerations comprise two or more bulleted points. Ideas relating to the reader appear first, followed by specific suggestions for a text-based task. Reader and Task considerations also appear embedded within the teaching notes as well as in the guiding question that opens each passage and in the comprehension questions. Keep in mind that Reader and Task considerations are the most variable of the three measures of text complexity. Reader issues relate to such broad concerns as prior knowledge and experience, cognitive abilities, reading skills, motivation by and engagement with the text, and content and/or theme concerns. Tasks are typically questions to answer, ideas to discuss, or activities to help students navigate and analyze the text, understand key ideas, and deepen comprehension. The same task may be stimulating for some students but daunting to others. Because you know your students best, use your judgment to adjust and revise tasks as appropriate.

Teaching Routine to Support Close Reading

Complex texts become more accessible to readers who are able to use various strategies during the reading process. One of the best ways to scaffold students through this process is to model a close-reading routine.

* **Preview the text.** Help students learn to identify clues about the meaning, purpose, or goal of the text. They can first read the title and the guiding question that precedes the passage. In literary texts, students can scan for characters' names and clues about setting and time frame. In informational texts, students can use features such as paragraph subheadings and supporting photos, illustrations, or other graphics to get a sense of the organization and purpose.

* **Quick-read to get the gist.** Have students do a "run-through" individual reading of the passage to get a sense of it. The quick-read technique can also help students identify areas of confusion or problem vocabulary. You can liken this step to scanning a new store to get a sense of how it is set up, what products it sells, and how you can find what you need.

* **Read closely.** Next, have students read the same piece again, this time with an eye to unlocking its deeper meaning or purpose. For most students, this is the time to use sticky notes, highlighter pens, margin notes, or graphic organizers to help them work their way through the important parts of the text. You might provide text-related graphic organizers, such as T-charts, compare/contrast and Venn diagrams, character and concept maps, cause-and-effect charts, or evidence/conclusion tables.

* **Respond to the text.** Now it's time for students to pull their ideas together and for you to assess their understanding. This may involve summarizing, reading aloud, holding group discussions, debates, or answering written questions. When you assign the after-reading question pages, suggest that students reread questions as needed before they attempt an answer. Encourage them to return to the text as well. Remind students to provide text-based evidence as part of every answer. Finally, consider with students the big ideas of a piece, its message, lesson, or purpose, and think about how to extend learning.

Above all, use the passages and teaching materials in this book to inspire students to become mindful readers—readers who delve deeply into a text to get the most out of it. Help your students recognize that reading is much more than just decoding all the words. Guide them to dig in, think about ideas, determine meaning, and grasp messages.

The following page presents two copies of a reproducible, six-step guide to mindful reading. It is intended as a reusable prompt. Students can keep it at hand to help them recall, apply, and internalize close-reading strategies whenever they read.

25 Complex Text Passages to Meet the Common Core: Literature and Informational Texts, Grade 2 © 2014 by Scholastic Teaching Resources

How to Be A Mindful Reader

Preview the text.

- What might it be about?

Read carefully.

- Stop to think as you read.
- Monitor your understanding.

Read again.

- You might notice new information.

Take notes.

- Circle the hard words.
- Write questions you may have.

Summarize.

- Jot down the main ideas.
- List the big events in order.

Think about it.

- What's the message?
- What ideas stand out?

How to Be A Mindful Reader

Preview the text.

- What might it be about?

Read carefully.

- Stop to think as you read.
- Monitor your understanding.

Read again.

- You might notice new information.

Take notes.

- Circle the hard words.
- Write questions you may have.

Summarize.

- Jot down the main ideas.
- List the big events in order.

Think about it.

- What's the message?
- What ideas stand out?

Connections to the Common Core State Standards

As shown in the chart below, the teaching resources in this book will help you meet many of the reading and language standards for grade 2 outlined in the CCSS. For details on these standards, visit the CCSS website: www.corestandards.org/the-standards/.

Passage	RL.2.1	RL.2.2	RL.2.3	RL.2.5	RL.2.6	RL.2.7	RL.2.10	RI.2.1	RI.2.2	RI.2.3	RI.2.4	RI.2.5	RI.2.6	RI.2.7	RI.2.8	RI.2.10	RF.2.3	RF.2.4	L.2.1	L.2.2	L.2.3	L.2.4	L.2.5	L.2.6
1	•	•	•	•	•	•	•										•	•	•	•	•	•	•	•
2	•	•	•	•	•	•	•										•	•	•	•	•	•	•	•
3	•	•	•	•		•	•										•	•	•	•	•	•	•	•
4	•	•	•	•		•	•										•	•	•	•	•	•	•	•
5	•	•	•	•	•	•	•										•	•	•	•	•	•	•	•
6	•	•	•	•	•	•	•										•	•	•	•	•	•	•	•
7	•	•	•	•		•	•										•	•	•	•	•	•	•	•
8	•	•	•	•	•	•	•										•	•	•	•	•	•	•	•
9	•	•	•	•	•	•	•										•	•	•	•	•	•	•	•
10								•	•		•	•	•	•	•	•	•	•	•	•	•	•	•	•
11								•	•		•	•	•			•	•	•	•	•	•	•	•	•
12								•	•	•	•	•	•		•	•	•	•	•	•	•	•	•	•
13								•	•		•	•	•		•	•	•	•	•	•	•	•	•	•
14								•	•		•	•	•		•	•	•	•	•	•	•	•	•	•
15								•	•	•	•	•	•	•		•	•	•	•	•	•	•	•	•
16								•	•		•	•	•	•		•	•	•	•	•	•	•	•	•
17								•	•		•	•	•	•			•	•	•	•	•	•	•	•
18								•	•	•	•	•	•			•	•	•	•	•	•	•	•	•
19								•	•		•	•	•	•	•	•	•	•	•	•	•	•	•	•
20								•	•		•	•	•				•	•	•	•	•	•	•	•
21								•	•		•	•	•	•	•	•	•	•	•	•	•	•	•	•
22								•	•		•	•	•	•		•	•	•	•	•	•	•	•	•
23								•	•	•	•	•	•	•	•	•	•	•	•	•	•	•	•	•
24								•	•	•	•	•	•	•	•	•	•	•	•	•	•	•	•	•
25								•	•		•	•	•	•	•	•	•	•	•	•	•	•	•	•

Passage 1   Raining Frogs? • page 26

Literature: Mystery

▶ **Focus** In this mystery that presents a puzzling event in nature, students practice identifying and reading dialogue.

▶ **Teaching Tips**

Before Reading

- Talk about what a mystery is. Invite students to give examples of mysteries they know.
- Discuss the title and the illustration. Encourage students to predict what this story will be about.

During Reading

- Guide readers to highlight vivid verbs as they read the mystery.
- Invite pairs to read the story aloud, alternating paragraphs. Guide students to notice the sentences in quotation marks and explain that this type of punctuation is a signal that someone is speaking. Encourage readers to use expression when reading dialogue.

After Reading

- Tell students that this fictional story is based on a true event that happened in 2005 in Odzaci, Serbia.
- Have students summarize the story in their own words. Encourage them to link Goran's illness with the strange sight of raining frogs.

Common Core Connections

RL.2.1, RL.2.2, RL.2.3, RL.2.5, RL.2.6, RL.2.7, RL.2.10 • RF.2.3, RF.2.4 • L.2.1, L.2.2, L.2.3, L.2.4, L.2.5, L.2.6

Complexity Index

Quantitative: Lexile 420

Qualitative	1	2	3	4	5
Meaning		✳			
Structure		✳			
Language		✳			
Knowledge		✳			

Reader & Task

- Students may be unfamiliar with the weather terms *heavy rain*, *windstorm*, and *tornado*.
- Challenge students to tell why Goran's mother wondered if he might be seeing things.

Passage 2   Sit, Stay, Read • page 28

Literature: Realistic Fiction

▶ **Focus** In this story, readers infer how a nonjudgmental visitor encourages a child to read aloud.

▶ **Teaching Tips**

Before Reading

- Pronounce each of the names that appear in this story. Highlight the silent *w* in *Wrigley*.
- Tell students that the real Sit-Stay-Read program began in Chicago schools to help children feel comfortable reading aloud. (Note: The name of this program is officially written as one word with initial capital letters, but it was changed in the student passage for easier readability.)

During Reading

- Ask students to study the illustration to figure out the meaning of the word *bandanna*.
- Challenge students to use context clues to figure out what the phrase, *noses a page*, in line 21 might mean.
- Point out to students that this story is written in the present tense.

After Reading

- Ask students to summarize the story and infer how reading aloud to Wrigley might help Zuri.

Common Core Connections

RL.2.1, RL.2.2, RL.2.3, RL.2.5, RL 2.6, RL.2.7, RL.2.10 • RF.2.3, RF.2.4 • L.2.1, L.2.2, L.2.3, L.2.4, L.2.5, L.2.6

Complexity Index

Quantitative: Lexile 460

Qualitative	1	2	3	4	5
Meaning	✳				
Structure		✳			
Language		✳			
Knowledge	✳				

Reader & Task

- Students may have difficulty pronouncing the proper names in the passage and may need prompting for the specific meanings of multiple-meaning words.
- Have students explain the purpose of the Sit-Stay-Read program and how it works in a classroom.

Literature: Fable

▶ **Focus** This Japanese fable asks readers to examine the character of a man who is never satisfied, and to predict what may happen next.

▶ **Teaching Tips**

Before Reading
- Talk about a fable as a simple story that teaches a life lesson. Invite students to suggest other fables they may know.
- Correctly pronounce for students the stonecutter's name as TAH-sah-koo.

During Reading
- Guide readers to notice irregular forms of verbs in the past tense, for example, *felt, wept, had, was, froze,* and *made.*
- Have students make a storyboard or timeline of the action.

After Reading
- Invite students to share the endings they wrote and discuss how each fits the lesson the fable hopes to teach.

Common Core Connections

RL.2.1, RL.2.2, RL.2.3, RL.2.5, RL.2.7, RL.2.10 • RF.2.3, RF.2.4 • L.2.1, L.2.2, L.2.3, L.2.4, L.2.5, L.2.6

Complexity Index

Quantitative: Lexile 470

Qualitative	1	2	3	4	5
Meaning			✳		
Structure			✳		
Language		✳			
Knowledge		✳			

Reader & Task

- Unlike Aesop's fables, this fable has no stated moral. Readers will have to infer from the story the lesson Tasaku will learn.
- Guide students in finding evidence in the text that helps answer the question that precedes the passage.

Literature: Historical Fiction

▶ **Focus** Students explore the genre of historical fiction in this story that presents surprising details of a very different and difficult way of life for some children of the past.

▶ **Teaching Tips**

Before Reading
- Discuss historical fiction. Examine the photo with students without revealing the theme of the story. Help them identify what the image shows and identify clues to the time period.

During Reading
- Encourage students to look for cause-and-effect relationships.
- Review unfamiliar vocabulary and mining terms (*moving belt, breaker boy, coal, slate*).
- Point out similes, such as *cold as an icebox* and *hot as an oven,* and discuss their meanings.

After Reading
- Challenge students to write questions they would ask Chet or his boss.
- Show students historic photographs taken by Lewis Hine (1874–1940) and explain that he tried to expose the hardships and injustice of child labor. Many can be found on the website of the Library of Congress.

Common Core Connections

RL.2.1, RL.2.2, RL.2.3, RL.2.5, RL.2.7, RL.2.10 • RF.2.3, RF.2.4 • L.2.1, L.2.2, L.2.3, L.2.4, L.2.5, L.2.6

Complexity Index

Quantitative: Lexile 510

Qualitative	1	2	3	4	5
Meaning		✳			
Structure	✳				
Language			✳		
Knowledge					✳

Reader & Task

- Students may have no knowledge that young children were once employed to do hard labor for long hours in dangerous conditions, in places such as mines.
- Encourage students to summarize Chet's daily life and routines, and note the ways his life differs the most from the lives and routines of most eight-year-olds today.

Literature: Myth

▶ **Focus** Students identify the style and elements of a "pourquoi" tale in this Native American Ojibwe myth.

▶ **Teaching Tips**

Before Reading

- Discuss how this myth is a pourquoi tale—a fictional story that tries to explain why animals look or behave as they do today because of something they did long ago.
- Correctly pronounce the name *Ojibwe* (oh-JEEB-weh). Tell students that the Ojibwe are a Native American people who still live on the American Great Plains. Also pronounce *Wenebojo* (weh-neh-BOH-zho). Explain that Wenebojo is a Native American spirit.

During Reading

- Tell readers to circle vivid action verbs that show movement, such as *poked, galloped, trampled, dashed,* and *raced.*
- Have students read the myth aloud. Encourage them to act out the parts when Wenebojo punished Buffalo and Fox to understand the use of the exclamation points.

After Reading

- Help students research the scientific reasons that explain why buffalo have humps and hang their heads low and why foxes live in holes in the ground.

Common Core Connections

RL.2.1, RL.2.2, RL.2.3, RL.2.5, RL 2.6, RL.2.7, RL.2.10 • RF.2.3, RF.2.4 • L.2.1, L.2.2, L.2.3, L.2.4, L.2.5, L.2.6

Complexity Index

Quantitative:
Lexile 530

Qualitative	1	2	3	4	5
Meaning		❊			
Structure		❊			
Language		❊			
Knowledge				❊	

Reader & Task

- Students may not know the habits of foxes and/or the physical appearance of the buffalo.
- As they read, encourage students to keep in mind the question that precedes the passage so that they can identify and discuss the cause-and-effect structure of the story.

Literature: Folktale

▶ **Focus** In this American folktale from Georgia, students identify how gentle humor is used to explain the origin of a regional expression.

▶ **Teaching Tips**

Before Reading

- Discuss some typical aspects of farm life, such as why farmers wake up early, what roosters do, or why farms set up scarecrows in their fields.
- Identify the state of Georgia on a map of the United States.

During Reading

- Have partners take turns reading the folktale aloud. Encourage them to *caw-n, cackle, crow,* and *gobble* to experience the meaning of onomatopoeic words.

After Reading

- Extend by asking students to write a thank-you note to the farmer, as if written by the satisfied crows. Or encourage them to add other farm animal characters to the tale.

Common Core Connections

RL.2.1, RL.2.2, RL.2.3, RL.2.5, RL.2.6, RL.2.7, RL.2.10 • RF.2.3, RF.2.4 • L.2.1, L.2.2, L.2.3, L.2.4, L.2.5, L.2.6

Complexity Index

Quantitative:
Lexile 550

Qualitative	1	2	3	4	5
Meaning		❊			
Structure	❊				
Language		❊			
Knowledge		❊			

Reader & Task

- Students may be unaware of regional differences in words, phrases, and expressions.
- Ask readers to explain in their own words what "the crows are in the corn" means without retelling the folktale.

Literature: Legend

▶ **Focus** This classic tale, based on an ancient Greek legend about unbridled greed, allows readers to make predictions and discuss how a character comes to realize the foolishness of his choice.

▶ **Teaching Tips**

Before Reading
- Talk about the meaning of the saying, "Be careful what you wish for."

During Reading
- Have students circle any unfamiliar words or phrases to discuss later.
- Tell readers to look for moments in the legend when they think Midas may be wondering whether he made a wise wish.

After Reading
- Work with students to craft a note from King Midas to the wizard. In the note, help them explain what went wrong with having the golden touch.

Common Core Connections

RL.2.1, RL.2.2, RL.2.3, RL.2.5, RL.2.7, RL.2.10 • RF.2.3, RF.2.4 • L.2.1, L.2.2, L.2.3, L.2.4, L.2.5, L.2.6

Complexity Index

Quantitative: Lexile 560

Qualitative	1	2	3	4	5
Meaning			✳		
Structure		✳			
Language		✳			
Knowledge		✳			

Reader & Task

- Some students may not be able to grasp the idea that getting what one wishes for may not always work out for the best.
- Have students contrast the character of King Midas as he was at the beginning of the legend with how he reacted by the end.

Literature: Humorous Fiction

▶ **Focus** This amusing story challenges students to infer an unexpectedly funny solution to a minor mystery.

▶ **Teaching Tips**

Before Reading
- Invite students to study the picture and predict what the story may be about.

During Reading
- Have readers describe the kind of person the storyteller is, based on text details.
- Tell students to notice text details that paint a picture of the dog and his behavior, for example, *he sniffed around*, *wagged his tail*, and *his legs made running movements, as if he was chasing rabbits in a dream.*

After Reading
- Ask students what the second note tells about Scooter's owner.
- Challenge students to rewrite the story from Scooter's point of view.

Common Core Connections

RL.2.1, RL.2.2, RL.2.3, RL.2.5, RL 2.6, RL.2.7, RL.2.10 • RF.2.3, RF.2.4 • L.2.1, L.2.2, L.2.3, L.2.4, L.2.5, L.2.6

Complexity Index

Quantitative: Lexile 590

Qualitative	1	2	3	4	5
Meaning		✳			
Structure		✳			
Language		✳			
Knowledge			✳		

Reader & Task

- Students may be unacquainted with typical dog behaviors; they may not know that many communities require dogs to be licensed and wear tags on their collars (for proof of ownership and vaccinations).
- Have readers use the information in the note on Scooter's collar, as well as Scooter's behavior, to describe his life and his family.

Literature: Fantasy

► **Focus** This passage exemplifies the features of a fantasy by describing a relationship between an imaginary creature and a real person. Students also connect details described in the text with a labeled illustration.

► **Teaching Tips**

Before Reading

- Read aloud the question that introduces the passage. Discuss the meaning of *fantasy* and the characteristics of an imaginary story.

During Reading

- Have readers circle compound words in the text (*grandmother, moonlight, dewdrops, cobwebs*).
- Tell students to link the information in the bulleted text with the body parts and labels on the illustration.

After Reading

- Invite students to use details from the text and illustration to write their own description of a unicorn. Encourage them to be as specific and thorough as possible.

Common Core Connections

RL.2.1, RL.2.2, RL.2.3, RL.2.5, RL 2.6, RL.2.7, RL.2.10 • RF.2.3, RF.2.4 • L.2.1, L.2.2, L.2.3, L.2.4, L.2.5, L.2.6

Complexity Index

Quantitative:
Lexile 620

Qualitative	1	2	3	4	5
Meaning			❋		
Structure				❋	
Language			❋		
Knowledge				❋	

Reader & Task

- Students may have trouble separating fact from fantasy, or recognizing that there is common sense within the fanciful description of good advice.
- Have students describe details in the story that help answer the question that precedes the passage.

Passage 10   Chinese Calendar • page 44

Informational Text: Cultural Article/Annotated Diagram

▶ **Focus** This article requires readers to gather information that is presented graphically with text details in accompanying captions.

▶ **Teaching Tips**

Before Reading

- Explain that the Chinese calendar describes a cycle of 12 years. Each animal is linked with an entire year, for example the year of the Tiger. (Note: Some versions of the calendar include alternatives for certain animals, for example, goat instead of sheep, and boar for pig.)

During Reading

- Instruct students to read about the Rat first, and then move clockwise around the wheel.
- Most of the text consists of adjectives. Have students circle ones they may not know.

After Reading

- Have students find out the birth year of each member of their family. Then help them research the animal linked with each birth year. Talk about how well each person fits his or her sign.

Common Core Connections

RI.2.1, RI.2.2, RI.2.4, RI.2.5, RI.2.6, RI.2.7, RI.2.8, RI.2.10 • RF.2.3, RF.2.4
• L.2.1, L.2.2, L.2.3, L.2.4, L.2.5, L.2.6

Complexity Index

Quantitative: Lexile 430

Qualitative	1	2	3	4	5
Purpose				✳	
Structure					✳
Language				✳	
Knowledge				✳	

Reader & Task

- Students from Chinese backgrounds may be able to offer additional information.
- Some students may have difficulty navigating the information as presented. (Note: In this passage, each section of captioned text is numbered, rather than individual lines of text.)
- Form groups of three or four students to play a kind of guessing game. In turn, each student asks a *Who am I?* question giving some or all of the traits of an animal in the Chinese calendar. Example: *I am chatty, well-liked, and skilled. Who am I?* (horse)

Passage 11   Word Wizard • page 46

Informational Text: Dictionary Entry

▶ **Focus** This selection presents students with a sample of a common reading challenge (multiple-meaning words) that can be solved by consulting a dictionary entry.

▶ **Teaching Tips**

Before Reading

- Present a list of easy-to-read, multiple-meaning words, such as *bat*, *count*, *hide*, or *jam*. Invite students to come up with sentences for each meaning of these words.

During Reading

- Before students read lines 10–20, discuss the format of the dictionary entry. Help them identify the kinds of information presented and the different styles used to organize the details.
- Explain to students that meanings are usually listed from most to least common.

After Reading

- Provide dictionaries to pairs of students. Present sentences that use a multiple-meaning word. Have pairs determine which of the meanings fits each usage.

Common Core Connections

RI.2.1, RI.2.2, RI.2.4, RI.2.5, RI.2.6, RI.2.10 •
RF.2.3, RF.2.4 • L.2.1, L.2.2, L.2.3, L.2.4, L.2.5, L.2.6

Complexity Index

Quantitative: Lexile 440

Qualitative	1	2	3	4	5
Purpose			✳		
Structure			✳		
Language			✳		
Knowledge			✳		

Reader & Task

- Students may not have had sufficient practice using a dictionary.
- Pair off students. Have one partner make up a sentence using any of the meanings of *mine*. The other partner identifies the correct meaning in that sentence. Then have partners switch roles.

Informational Text: Speech

▶ **Focus** Students read a speech that presents one person's point of view with supporting examples

▶ **Teaching Tips**

Before Reading

● Preview with students two key words: *superstition* and *triskaidekaphobia*. Pronounce them together, but tell students they will learn the meanings by reading a speech.

During Reading

● Point out different text features, for example, words in italics (lines 8 and 16), a sentence in brackets (line 16), and words or word parts in capital letters (lines 17–18, and 25). Ask students to explain the use of each one.

After Reading

● Have students present short speeches to classmates about a new long word—*not* from passage—they have learned.

● Help students learn to read and pronounce other long words with interesting meanings.

Common Core Connections

RI.2.1, RI.2.2, RI.2.3, RI.2.4, RI.2.5, RI.2.6, RI.2.8, RI.2.10 • RF.2.3, RF.2.4 • L.2.1, L.2.2, L.2.3, L.2.4, L.2.5, L.2.6

Complexity Index

Quantitative: Lexile 450

Qualitative	1	2	3	4	5
Purpose		✳			
Structure		✳			
Language			✳		
Knowledge		✳			

Reader & Task

● Some students may not understand that superstitions are not based in fact.

● Have students describe how superstitions mentioned by the speaker affect people's behaviors.

Informational Text: Interview

▶ **Focus** Students read an informational interview and identify its features.

▶ **Teaching Tips**

Before Reading

● Talk about what an interview is. Then guide students to notice the question-and-answer structure and how it differs from other types of writing.

During Reading

● Point out text features used in the interview: names in boldface, questions in italics, and answers in regular type. Discuss how these features help the reader distinguish between the interview participants.

● Have students work in pairs to role-play Rico and Wanda reading the interview aloud.

After Reading

● Invite students to share the questions they wrote for item 4 on page 51.

Common Core Connections

RI.2.1, RI.2.2, RI.2.4, RI.2.5, RI.2.6, RI.2.8, RI.2.10 • RF.2.3, RF.2.4 • L.2.1, L.2.2, L.2.3, L.2.4, L.2.5, L.2.6

Complexity Index

Quantitative: Lexile 460

Qualitative	1	2	3	4	5
Purpose		✳			
Structure			✳		
Language		✳			
Knowledge		✳			

Reader & Task

● Students who do not travel by school bus may be unacquainted with some of the ideas.

● Have students use the passage as a model for interviewing an adult they know about that person's job and share the results with the class.

Informational Text: Safety Poster

▶ **Focus** Written in an easy-to-follow question-and-answer format, this poster provides students with basic guidelines for using an important public service.

▶ **Teaching Tips**

Before Reading
- Point out the format of the piece: The information is presented in the form of boldface questions with answers that are indented. How might the format aid in comprehension?

During Reading
- Direct attention to the leading words in the questions: *What, When, Who, Why, How.* Also point out the use of all capital letters for emphasis (FREE, FAST, ONLY).
- Tell readers to jot down questions or points to discuss beside each response.

After Reading
- Discuss with students the seriousness of dialing 9-1-1. Then brainstorm to generate a list of emergency situations and have groups role-play making and answering 9-1-1 calls. Encourage students to follow the guidelines presented on the poster.

Common Core Connections

RI.2.1, RI.2.2, RI.2.4, RI.2.5, RI.2.6, RI.2.8, RI.2.10 • RF.2.3, RF.2.4 • L.2.1, L.2.2, L.2.3, L.2.4, L.2.5, L.2.6

Complexity Index

Quantitative: Lexile 470

Qualitative	1	2	3	4	5
Purpose	✴				
Structure			✴		
Language		✴			
Knowledge		✴			

Reader & Task

- Students may be familiar with the existence of the 9-1-1 emergency service, but may never have used it or seen it used.
- Have students explain how the poster's features makes it easy to find information and why this is especially useful for a topic like 9-1-1.

Informational Text: Procedural/Science Activity

▶ **Focus** In this "how-to" piece, students read a set of simple instructions that includes a bulleted list of materials, a numbered list of steps to follow, subheadings that distinguish the two, and supporting art.

▶ **Teaching Tips**

Before Reading
- Elicit prior knowledge about following recipes, directions, experiments, or projects that involve some materials and a series of steps.
- Guide readers to recognize that the piece has three main parts: an introduction, a list of materials, and a numbered list of steps to follow.

During Reading
- Ask students why it's important to read the entire set of instructions and ask any questions they may have *before* attempting to make the paint.
- Suggest that students link the materials to the steps that use them.

After Reading
- Have students work in small groups to follow the steps in order to make and try out the paint. Afterward, invite them to discuss how things went.

Common Core Connections

RI.2.1, RI.2.2, RI.2.3, RI.2.4, RI.2.5, RI.2.6, RI.2.7, RI.2.10 • RF.2.3, RF.2.4 • L.2.1, L.2.2, L.2.3, L.2.4, L.2.5, L.2.6

Complexity Index

Quantitative: Lexile 480

Qualitative	1	2	3	4	5
Purpose		✴			
Structure				✴	
Language		✴			
Knowledge			✴		

Reader & Task

- Some students may find this layout (with its assorted text features and structures) challenging to read.
- Help students understand why the text is broken down into parts and sequential steps by asking how the outcome might change if the steps were not in order.

Informational Text: Data Article/Table

▶ **Focus** This article presents data about time in paragraph form, in a table, with an illustration, and with a mnemonic device readers can apply.

▶ **Teaching Tips**

Before Reading

- Ask: *What is time?* Develop an idea web based on students' responses. Discuss how we notice time, talk about it, record it, why we use it, and so on.

During Reading

- Guide readers to notice various text features: italics, boldface text, caption, and data table.
- If possible, set a sand timer clock as students begin to read, and keep track of how many times you must flip it until everyone finishes.

After Reading

- Have students write descriptive sentences using the time words listed in Reader & Task. They can draw pictures to accompany their writing. Post their work on a display entitled "It's About Time!"

Common Core Connections

RI.2.1, RI.2.2, RI.2.4, RI.2.5, RI.2.6, RI.2.7, RI.2.8, RI.2.10 • RF.2.3, RF.2.4
• L.2.1, L.2.2, L.2.3, L.2.4, L.2.5, L.2.6

Complexity Index

Quantitative:
Lexile 540

Qualitative	1	2	3	4	5
Purpose				✳	
Structure					✳
Language			✳		
Knowledge			✳		

Reader & Task

- Most students have had extensive experience with the broad concept of time, but may not have considered it in some of the ways presented and described in this piece.
- Have students demonstrate understanding of the time words used in the piece: *yesterday, today, tomorrow, before, now, later.*

Informational Text: Biographical Sketch

▶ **Focus** This biographical sketch, based primarily on the subject's own words, offers students first-hand information about his life and work.

▶ **Teaching Tips**

Before Reading

- Discuss with students the distinctions between a book's author and its illustrator. Point out that some people both write and illustrate their books.

During Reading

- Have readers use a highlighter pen to indicate the words that Jerry Pinkney himself said.
- Encourage students to use context clues to explain the meaning of the words *realized* (line 9) and *focuses* (line 21).

After Reading

- Read aloud several books illustrated by Jerry Pinkney. For each book, first tell students to focus on the cover illustration. Encourage them to describe the details they observe and to predict what the book might be about. Then reread the first line of the passage and ask students to explain why the writer includes Jerry Pinkney's quote that he is a "storyteller at heart."

Common Core Connections

RI.2.1, RI.2.2, RI.2.4, RI.2.6, RI.2.7, RI.2.8, RI.2.10 • RF.2.3, RF.2.4 • L.2.1, L.2.2, L.2.3, L.2.4, L.2.5, L.2.6

Complexity Index

Quantitative:
Lexile 560

Qualitative	1	2	3	4	5
Purpose			✳		
Structure			✳		
Language			✳		
Knowledge		✳			

Reader & Task

- Students may be unaccustomed to learning about a person based on direct quotations.
- Students who find reading challenging will relate to Jerry Pinkney's early experiences in school.
- Guide students to pick out quotations from the passage and explain what they tell about Jerry Pinkney.

Informational Text: Procedural/Technical Process

▶ **Focus** In this procedural piece, students use text and supporting pictures to understand the major steps in a complex technical process.

▶ **Teaching Tips**

Before Reading

- Distribute coins of any denomination for students to examine and describe. Ask: *Where do coins come from?* List their answers.

During Reading

- Encourage students to do repeated readings of the piece to assimilate all the information and answer the questions. Guide them to examine the supporting illustrations for each step as an aid to comprehension.
- Discuss multiple-meaning words in the text (for example, *mint, place, steps, punches, sheets, disks, stamps, striking, check*).

After Reading

- Challenge students to respond to the piece by discussing and/or writing about how the illustrations helped them follow the steps of the minting process.

Common Core Connections

RI.2.1, RI.2.2, RI.2.3, RI.2.4, RI.2.5, RI.2.6, RI.2.7, RI.2.10 • RF.2.3, RF.2.4 • L.2.1, L.2.2, L.2.3, L.2.4, L.2.5, L.2.6

Complexity Index

Quantitative: Lexile 570

Qualitative	1	2	3	4	5
Purpose				✳	
Structure					✳
Language					✳
Knowledge					✳

Reader & Task

- This essay presents a great deal of new information, specific details, and includes many multiple-meaning words.
- Prepare a sequencing activity to check for comprehension: Copy each of the six steps onto a different index card, but omit the numbers. Shuffle the cards and challenge students to arrange them in the correct order.

Informational Text: Language Arts Essay/Idioms

▶ **Focus** This lighthearted essay encourages readers to think about the meanings of common idiomatic expressions.

▶ **Teaching Tips**

Before Reading

- Present a common idiom or two to discuss (for example, *break the ice; a piece of cake*). Point out that the specific words in an idiom often mean something different when used together than they do when used alone.

During Reading

- Point out how the use of italics in the passage highlights each idiom.
- Encourage reading partners to talk about each paragraph together to help them grasp the meaning of the given idiom.

After Reading

- Have students write a real-life example that would match the idioms used in this essay. It may help to offer an example of your own to model for students.

Common Core Connections

RI.2.1, RI.2.2, RI.2.4, RI.2.5, RI.2.6, RI.2.7, RI.2.8, RI.2.10 • RF.2.3, RF.2.4 • L.2.1, L.2.2, L.2.3, L.2.4, L.2.5, L.2.6

Complexity Index

Quantitative: Lexile 580

Qualitative	1	2	3	4	5
Purpose			✳		
Structure		✳			
Language					✳
Knowledge				✳	

Reader & Task

- English Language Learners may have difficulty interpreting idioms because they are usually not literal.
- List each of the six idioms used in the essay. Have students explain the meaning of each one.

Informational Text: Persuasive Essay

▶ **Focus** This passage offers students an example of a persuasive essay that considers opposing arguments before suggesting a compromise solution.

▶ **Teaching Tips**

Before Reading
- Explain what it means to *persuade* (argue for, convince, win over by facts and details). Present the adjectival form *persuasive* to introduce this type of essay.

During Reading
- Encourage students to highlight the topic sentence in each paragraph.

After Reading
- Have students respond in writing to the essay by adding other reasons for or against riding bikes to school.

Common Core Connections

RI.2.1, RI.2.2, RI.2.4, RI.2.5, RI.2.6, RI.2.7, RI.2.8, RI.2.10 • RF.2.3, RF.2.4 • L.2.1, L.2.2, L.2.3, L.2.4, L.2.5, L.2.6

Complexity Index

Quantitative: Lexile 590

Qualitative	1	2	3	4	5
Purpose				✳	
Structure			✳		
Language			✳		
Knowledge		✳			

Reader & Task

- Most students will be engaged by the topic of riding bicycles, and some may be familiar with the concerns raised in the essay.
- Encourage students to explain how the organization of the essay helps the writer make his or her points effectively.

Informational Text: Social Studies Essay

▶ **Focus** This essay explores a grade-appropriate civics concept through text, a numbered list, italics, boldface text, and a representative graphic.

▶ **Teaching Tips**

Before Reading
- Display the words *citizen*, *community*, *neighbor*, *right*, and *responsibility*. Help students read and pronounce these words, and tell what they know about the terms. Focus on *citizen* as it applies to being part of a community (for example, neighborhood, classroom, family, club).

During Reading
- You may wish to read the essay aloud as students follow along. Pause frequently to discuss key vocabulary and ideas or answer students' questions. Then have students reread independently.

After Reading
- Have small groups reread the essay and discuss the steps of good citizenship. Then ask students to cite specific examples that demonstrate each step.

Common Core Connections

RI.2.1, RI.2.2, RI.2.4, RI.2.5, RI.2.6, RI.2.7, RI.2.8, RI.2.10 • RF.2.3, RF.2.4 • L.2.1, L.2.2, L.2.3, L.2.4, L.2.5, L.2.6

Complexity Index

Quantitative: Lexile 610

Qualitative	1	2	3	4	5
Purpose				✳	
Structure			✳		
Language			✳		
Knowledge			✳		

Reader & Task

- For many students, the term *citizen* may be confusing, or even controversial.
- Guide readers to focus on the steps any good citizen can follow and explain how each is important for a community to thrive.

Informational Text: Music Essay/Chart

▶ **Focus** Students compare and contrast string instruments using text and an informational chart with photographs.

▶ **Teaching Tips**

Before Reading
- Distribute rubber bands to students so they can stretch and pluck them to make vibrations. Have them try for different "notes" by changing lengths and tension.

During Reading
- Have students first scan the page to get a sense of its topic and organization. Guide them to read and reread to assimilate as much information as possible.
- Help students navigate the chart, as needed. Go row by row *and* column by column.

After Reading
- Tell students that the piano is in the string family, too. Show a video that reveals the inner workings of a piano to help students determine how its strings vibrate.

Common Core Connections

RI.2.1, RI.2.2, RI.2.4, RI.2.5, RI.2.6, RI.2.7, RI.2.8, RI.2.10 ● RF.2.3, RF.2.4
● L.2.1, L.2.2, L.2.3, L.2.4, L.2.5, L.2.6

Complexity Index

Quantitative: Lexile 620

Qualitative	1	2	3	4	5
Purpose				✳	
Structure				✳	
Language					✳
Knowledge				✳	

Reader & Task

- Some students may have difficulty classifying, comparing, and contrasting. Others may have little or no familiarity with musical instruments.
- Encourage students to highlight evidence in the text to help them in answering the questions on page 69.

Informational Text: Earth Science Article

▶ **Focus** This essay uses boldface subheadings, italics, text examples, and photographs to explain cause-and-effect relationships in the natural world.

▶ **Teaching Tips**

Before Reading
- Mound some sand in a bowl. Then gently blow air through a straw at the sand as students watch. Talk about what happened (*mound of sand changed shape, holes may have appeared*). Introduce the word *erosion*.

During Reading
- Clarify that the term *weathering* comes from the word *weather*, showing that weather is an active force that causes change. Use the phrase to *weather away*.
- Encourage students to use the photos to help them visualize each type of weathering.

After Reading
- Perform another weathering demonstration that shows how water expands when it freezes. Fill a clear plastic bottle almost to the top with water. Mark the water level on the outside of the bottle. Then place it in a freezer until the water is frozen solid. As the water freezes, it expands, causing some of the ice to extend out of the top. Have students write a "lab report" about what happened.

Common Core Connections

RI.2.1, RI.2.2, RI.2.3, RI.2.4, RI.2.5, RI.2.6, RI.2.7, RI.2.8, RI.2.10 ● RF.2.3, RF.2.4
● L.2.1, L.2.2, L.2.3, L.2.4, L.2.5, L.2.6

Complexity Index

Quantitative: Lexile 630

Qualitative	1	2	3	4	5
Purpose				✳	
Structure				✳	
Language					✳
Knowledge				✳	

Reader & Task

- Students may not realize how much the earth experiences natural changes over time.
- Check for comprehension by asking students to use evidence from the text to explain the meaning of the last sentence in the first paragraph: *Nature itself can change rocks.*

Informational Text: Museum Review

▶ **Focus** Students read an example of the kind of review visitors might consult before planning a trip.

▶ **Teaching Tips**

Before Reading

• Inform students that there are many small museums in the world that focus on one subject, such as checkers, lunchboxes, rope, or mustard! Brainstorm collections that might be displayed in one-subject museums.

During Reading

• Point out the boldface subheadings as an organizational tool.

• Encourage students to notice the different kinds of information the review presents.

After Reading

• Invite students to use the review as a model to write their own review of an interesting place in their community.

Common Core Connections

RI.2.1, RI.2.2, RI.2.3, RI.2.4, RI.2.5, RI.2.6, RI.2.7, RI.2.8, RI.2.10 • RF.2.3, RF.2.4 • L.2.1, L.2.2, L.2.3, L.2.4, L.2.5, L.2.6

Complexity Index

Quantitative: Lexile 640

Qualitative	1	2	3	4	5
Purpose			✳		
Structure			✳		
Language				✳	
Knowledge				✳	

Reader & Task

• Though most students know about museums, few will realize that writers often describe museums to help people decide whether to visit them.

• Ask students to cite details the writer uses to attract readers of the review to the museum.

Informational Text: Postcard

▶ **Focus** Students read a postcard that contains a group message to a family member back home. They then use text clues to determine the writer of each paragraph.

▶ **Teaching Tips**

Before Reading

• Show examples of postcards. Explain that many postcards have a picture on the front and room to write a message on the back. Review the format for writing a mailing address.

• Ask students what they notice about each paragraph on the postcard and what this might mean.

During Reading

• Tell readers to highlight any clues that help them figure out the writer of each paragraph. You might ask questions to help them determine who *didn't* write a section.

After Reading

• Provide completely blank postcards (or facsimiles of them). Invite students to draw a picture on one side and then write to someone about the image on the reverse side. Help them address it in proper form.

Common Core Connections

RI.2.1, RI.2.2, RI.2.4, RI.2.5, RI.2.6, RI.2.7, RI.2.8, RI.2.10 • RF.2.3, RF.2.4 • L.2.1, L.2.2, L.2.3, L.2.4, L.2.5, L.2.6

Complexity Index

Quantitative: Lexile 650

Qualitative	1	2	3	4	5
Purpose			✳		
Structure				✳	
Language			✳		
Knowledge			✳		

Reader & Task

• Students may never have written or received a postcard; some may have trouble recognizing the clues that can help them determine who wrote each paragraph.

• Challenge students to explain how they determined which person wrote each paragraph to answer the question that precedes the passage.

Name _____ Date _____

Raining Frogs?

What is odd about what Goran sees?

1   Winds blew dark clouds across
2   the sky. Goran, in bed with the flu,
3   watched from his window. He expected
4   heavy rain. But instead of water, he
5   saw tiny frogs falling!
6   Goran wondered if fever made him
7   see things. He called for his mother,
8   who hurried in. "Mama, can it rain
9   frogs?" he asked.
10   His mother touched his hot
11 forehead. "Your fever makes you dream
12 things. I will bring you cold water to help you feel better."
13   On her way to the kitchen, Mama stopped. She saw tiny
14 frogs hopping everywhere outside. They were crossing the
15 road, jumping on the porch, and leaping in her garden.
16 People were out looking at the frogs. Mama called, "Are
17 they real?"
18   "Yes!" one said. "This is a windstorm. Winds can spin
19 very fast, like a tornado. These winds probably passed over
20 ponds with baby frogs in them. The wind sucked up the
21 water and the frogs in it. When the wind calmed down,
22 everything fell from the sky. So we did have falling frogs!"
23   Mama returned to Goran's room. "Darling, your
24 forehead is warm but your eyes are clear. You did see frogs
25 falling like rain."

Name _____ Date _____

Raining Frogs?

▶ **Answer each question. Give evidence from the mystery.**

1 Why is Goran in bed (line 2)?

○ A. He cannot walk.   ○ C. He wants to see frogs.

○ B. He doesn't feel well.   ○ D. He likes to read in bed.

What helped you pick your answer? _____

_____

_____

2 Which best describes how a tornado moves?

○ A. It flashes.   ○ B. It leaps.   ○ C. It rumbles.   ○ D. It twirls.

How did you pick your answer? _____

_____

_____

3 Why did Mama touch Goran's forehead (lines 10 and 11)? _____

_____

_____

4 Why is this story a mystery? Explain. _____

_____

_____

_____

Name _____ Date _____

Sit, Stay, Read

What is the meaning of the title?

1   It's Zuri's day to read to
2   Wrigley. Wrigley is a dog in
3   the Sit-Stay-Read program. He
4   knows to stay quietly beside
5   Zuri as she reads. Zuri has read
6   this week's book many times
7   and knows all the hard words.
8   Soon a wet black nose
9   appears at the door. It's
10 Wrigley! He enters with his
11 owner. Wrigley wears a green
12 bandanna. Zuri shakes Mr. Lim's hand and tickles
13 Wrigley under his chin. She leads her guests to a cozy
14 corner. Wrigley sits on a folded towel. Zuri sits beside
15 him, with Mr. Lim nearby.
16   "Thanks for coming, Wrigley. Today I will read you
17 *Why Is Blue Dog Blue*? I'll show the pictures, too." The dog
18 lies down, and Zuri begins.
19   Even if Zuri misses a word, Wrigley still listens. Zuri
20 describes the pictures to him and links them to the story.
21 She grins when Wrigley noses a page. But she never
22 worries about reading to Wrigley because he is so patient.
23   After she finishes, Zuri cups one hand. Mr. Lim puts a
24 dog treat in it. Zuri holds the treat near Wrigley. "Great
25 listening, Wrigley. Good dog!"

Name _____ Date _____

Sit, Stay, Read

▶ **Answer each question. Give evidence from the story.**

1 Who is Mr. Lim?

○ A. He is a dog.   ○ C. He is Zuri's teacher.

○ B. He is an author.   ○ D. He is Wrigley's owner.

What helped you pick your answer? _____

_____

_____

2 Which word best describes Wrigley?

○ A. wet   ○ B. hungry   ○ C. patient   ○ D. ticklish

How did you pick your answer? _____

_____

_____

3 Explain what Zuri tries to do for Wrigley when she *links* the pictures
to the story (lines 19 and 20).

_____

_____

4 Describe what might make a corner *cozy* (lines 13 and 14). _____

_____

_____

Name _____ Date _____

The Stonecutter
Fable From Japan

What lesson does this fable try to teach?

1   Tasaku was a stonecutter.
2   He worked hard for his good
3   life. One day a prince rode
4   by. Tasaku wept with envy
5   because he wished to be a
6   prince and have a better life.
7   The mountain spirit
8   granted Tasaku's wish. Tasaku
9   became a prince. His life was
10 better. One day, he saw that
11 the sun burned the flowers in his garden. This made Tasaku
12 realize that the sun was stronger than a prince. Filled with
13 envy, he begged the mountain spirit to make him the sun.
14   So it was. As the sun, Tasaku had an even better life. He
15 began to show off. He baked the land and made creatures
16 beg for water. When a cloud covered him, Tasaku saw that
17 a cloud was stronger than the sun. He begged the mountain
18 spirit to turn him into a cloud.
19   Tasaku the cloud enjoyed his better life. He caused storms
20 that froze and flooded the land. But he wanted still more. "To
21 be truly happy, I must be a mountain!" Tasaku complained.
22   The mountain spirit granted that last wish. Tasaku the
23 mountain felt stronger than the prince, the sun, and the
24 cloud. But inside he was lonely. One day, he felt a stonecutter
25 tapping at his base…

Name _____ Date _____

The Stonecutter

▶ **Answer each question. Give evidence from the fable.**

1 What was the first thing Tasaku wished for?

○ A. He wished to be a mountain.   ○ C. He wished to be the sun.

○ B. He wished to be a prince.   ○ D. He wished to be a cloud.

What helped you pick your answer? _____

_____

2 Which could be a different title for this fable?

○ A. Show Off When You Get Lucky   ○ C. Be Happy With What You Have

○ B. The Kind and Loving Tasaku   ○ D. Mountain Spirits Are Powerful

How did you pick your answer? _____

_____

_____

3 What is the meaning of *envy* (lines 4 and 13)? Explain. _____

_____

_____

4 The last sentence ends with (...). What do you think will happen next? Tell why.

_____

_____

Name _____ Date _____

Breaker Boy

How can you tell that Chet lived long ago?

1   Chet was eight years old. He told the boss he was 12
2   and small for his age. Everybody knew that was a lie. But
3   that lie got him a job as a breaker boy.
4   Chet woke up every day at five, ate a biscuit, and put
5   on his dusty clothes. He walked for an hour to get to the
6   mine. He had to be on his wood bench by seven. The
7   breaker room was as hot as an oven in summer. It was as
8   cold as an icebox in winter. The air was dirty all year long.
9   Chunks of coal mixed with other materials passed
10 below Chet's feet on a moving belt. He and the others
11 picked out anything that wasn't coal. It might be clumps
12 of clay, slabs of slate, or plain rocks. It was boring and
13 dangerous work. But it earned him money.
14 Chet's filthy hands were red with scrapes and cuts.
15 Gloves were not allowed. His back, neck, and arms were
16 sore from bending
17 all day. But what
18 choice was there? He,
19 Ma, and the babies
20 needed money. So no
21 more school for Chet.
22 No more farm work
23 either. Just long, hard
24 days of work.

Breaker boys at work

Name _____ Date _____

Breaker Boy

▶ **Answer each question. Give evidence from the story.**

1 What was the breaker room like in summer?

○ A. It was rocky and dark.   ○ C. It was cool and calm.

○ B. It was way too hot.   ○ D. It was warm and cozy.

What helped you pick your answer? _____

_____

_____

2 Why did Chet lie about his age?

○ A. He was too young for the job he needed.

○ B. He liked working with older boys.

○ C. He was ashamed he was so small.

○ D. He wanted to miss school.

How did you choose your answer? _____

_____

3 Explain the job of a breaker boy. _____

_____

_____

4 Look closely at the photo. Tell how it fits Chet's story. _____

_____

_____

Name _____ Date _____

Wenebojo Gets Angry
Ojibwe Myth

Why does Wenebojo change Buffalo and Fox?

1 In the beginning, Wenebojo kept watch over all
2 animals. Buffalo had no hump then, and Fox lived in the
3 trees. Buffalo ran over the fields to have fun on warm days.
4 Fox raced ahead of Buffalo to warn small animals that he
5 was coming.
6 But Fox didn't notice the tiny birds that made nests on
7 the ground. Buffalo galloped hard and trampled the nests.
8 The birds begged Buffalo to be kind but Buffalo paid no
9 attention.
10 The birds kept crying about their broken nests.
11 Wenebojo took pity. He made Buffalo and Fox stand before
12 him. Buffalo hung his head and humped his shoulders.
13 Wenebojo poked Buffalo in the shoulders with a stick. Fox
14 dashed away. He dug a hole in the ground to hide.
15 Wenebojo stared at Buffalo and said, "Shame! Shame
16 on you, Buffalo! From now on, you will always have a
17 hump on your back. You will hang your head low in
18 shame forever."
19 Then Wenebojo called to Fox.
20 "Shame on you, Fox! From now on,
21 you will live in the cold ground.
22 This is because you did not warn
23 the little birds."
24 So buffaloes have humps and
25 foxes live in the ground to this day.

25 Complex Text Passages to Meet the Common Core: Literature and Informational Texts, Grade 2 © 2014 by Scholastic Teaching Resources

Name _____ Date _____

Wenebojo Gets Angry

▶ **Answer each question. Give evidence from the myth.**

1 Who was Wenebojo?

○ A. the spirit who looked after
the animals

○ C. the leader of
the tiny birds

○ B. the strongest animal in the world

○ D. the king of the fields

What helped you pick your answer? _____

_____

_____

2 What made Wenebojo angry with Fox?

○ A. Fox lived in the trees.

○ C. Fox dug a hole in the ground.

○ B. Fox trampled the nests.

○ D. Fox didn't warn the tiny birds.

How did you pick your answer? _____

_____

3 How does the picture support the story? _____

_____

_____

4 How can we tell that Buffalo knew he had done wrong? _____

_____

_____

Name _____ Date _____

Crows in the Corn
Folktale From Georgia

How do you know that this story is a folktale?

1   A Georgia farmer slept late one morning because
2   she needed extra rest. This was very odd. The crows met
3   nearby, but saw no people to chase them away. They also
4   saw a field of ripe corn. So they flew right to that field to
5   feast. "Caw-n! Caw-n!" they cackled.

6   Their noise awoke the rooster, who crowed, "Wake
7   up! Wake up!" The farmer tossed and turned, but kept
8   sleeping as the crows ate her corn.

9   The rooster crowed louder. "Crows are in the corn!
10   Crows are in the corn!" But the farmer slept on. The
11   rooster tried again and again to wake the farmer, but she
12   still slept. So the rooster finally gave up trying.

13   Then a turkey came by to watch the crows feasting.
14   Soon she gobbled, "The corn is all gone."

15   Later the farmer woke up at last and went outside.
16   She saw that her corn was all gone, but she didn't see a
17   single crow. So when Georgia folks say "the crows are in
18   the corn," they mean that it's time to get up!

25 Complex Text Passages to Meet the Common Core: Literature and Informational Texts, Grade 2 © 2014 by Scholastic Teaching Resources

Name _____ Date _____

Crows in the Corn

▶ **Answer each question. Give evidence from the folktale.**

1 What did the farmer do that was odd?

○ A. She slept very late.   ○ C. She didn't see any crows.

○ B. She planted a field of corn.   ○ D. She tossed and turned.

What helped you pick your answer? _____

_____

_____

2 Corn that is *ripe* (line 4) _____.

○ A. smells bad   ○ C. is ready to eat

○ B. looks green   ○ D. wakes up roosters

How did you pick your answer? _____

_____

_____

3 Why were the crows able to feast on so much corn? _____

_____

4 Why did the author write *Caw-n* (line 5) for the sound the crows made? Explain.

_____

_____

Name _____ Date _____

The Golden Touch

Legend From Greece

What happens in the story to change King Midas?

1 Long ago lived a rich man called King
2 Midas. He was richer than anyone on
3 Earth. Still, he always wanted more.

4 One day, a wizard granted King Midas
5 one wish. "May all that I touch turn to
6 gold!" At once, his wish came true.

7 King Midas loved his new power. He
8 spent all day touching things. He turned
9 flowers, trees, and rocks into gold. He
10 turned tables and chairs into gold. Midas
11 was giddy with golden delight.

12 That night, King Midas sat on his golden throne and
13 called for supper. He took a red apple. But before he could
14 bite into it, it turned to gold. He tried to eat some bread,
15 but it turned to gold. He drank from a gold goblet, but the
16 water in it turned to gold as it touched his lips. Midas went
17 to bed hungry.

18 The next day, the king's daughter came to him for her
19 morning hug. Before Midas realized what would happen,
20 his touch turned her into a gold statue. "NO MORE!" Midas
21 cried. "What use is gold without my sweet girl? I don't want
22 this golden touch anymore!"

23 The wizard appeared and turned everything gold back
24 into what it was before. King Midas hugged his daughter,
25 and the two shared a huge breakfast.

Name _____ Date _____

The Golden Touch

▶ **Answer each question. Give evidence from the legend.**

1 What made Midas want to end his golden touch?

○ A. It was hard turning things into gold.   ○ C. He grew bored with gold.

○ B. He turned his daughter into a statue.   ○ D. He couldn't eat or drink.

What helped you pick your answer? _____

_____

_____

2 When King Midas felt *giddy* (line 11), he felt _____.

○ A. joyful   ○ B. bright   ○ C. worried   ○ D. ashamed

How did you pick your answer? _____

_____

_____

3 Why was Midas foolish to wish for a golden touch? _____

_____

_____

4 Why did King Midas have such a big breakfast (lines 24 and 25)?

_____

_____

_____

Name _____ Date _____

The Napping Dog

What are some funny things about this story?

1 One afternoon a gray dog wandered into our yard.

2 He sniffed around and then lay down. Since he wore

3 a collar and tags, we thought that he probably was

4 making a visit.

5 We don't have a dog, so my sister and I went out for

6 a closer look. The dog lifted his head and wagged his

7 tail. He then followed us back inside, curled up on a rug,

8 and fell asleep. His legs made running movements, as if

9 he was chasing rabbits in a dream.

10 After an hour, the dog woke up, stretched, and stood

11 by the door. I let him out and off he went. The next day,

12 he returned at the same time, and we followed the same

13 routine. This kept up for almost three weeks, but we still

14 didn't know whose dog he was.

15 So I tied a note to his collar. It said, "Who owns this

16 sweet dog? Did you know he visits us for a nap almost

17 every day?"

18 The next day, there was

19 the dog in our yard again,

20 but with a new note tied to

21 his collar. "This is Scooter.

22 His family has five kids, all

23 younger than seven. Scooter

24 just needs some rest. Can I

25 join him tomorrow?"

Name _____ Date _____

The Napping Dog

▶ **Answer each question. Give evidence from the story.**

1 Which of these is a routine most children follow?

○ A. reading a map   ○ C. visiting the moon

○ B. giving a speech   ○ D. brushing their teeth

What helped you pick your answer? _____

_____

_____

2 Who wrote the second note (lines 21–25)?

○ A. Scooter   ○ C. Scooter's owner

○ B. the dog catcher   ○ D. one of the five young children

How did you choose your answer? _____

_____

_____

3 Why does the person telling the story think that the dog has an owner?

_____

_____

4 Why would Scooter need rest away from his family? _____

_____

_____

Name _____ Date _____

Unicorn Secrets

What makes this story a fantasy?

1   Do you believe in unicorns? Most people say that
2 unicorns aren't real, so you probably don't. But when my
3 grandmother was nine, she met a unicorn in the woods one
4 summer night. Both were scared and shy, but they became
5 friends. My grandmother learned these unicorn secrets,
6 which she shared with me.
7 ● Swim every night in fresh cold water. This keeps your
8   horn and coat clean so they can shine in the moonlight.
9 ● Sip goat's milk and dewdrops. These liquids give you
10   powerful legs and tough teeth.
11 ● Eat fresh cobwebs every day. They help your mane and
12   tail to grow silky and strong.
13 ● Run along a sandy beach or rocky trail every day.
14   Your hooves and your balance will become sturdy.
15 ● Look deeply into someone's eyes to find his or her true
16   feelings. Eyes never lie.
17 ● Pick your friends with care.
18   Choose only those who will
19   always be kind and true.
20   As for me, I don't believe
21 in unicorns at all. Still, I
22 think that my grandmother
23 got some very good advice
24 somehow!

horn   mane   tail   coat   hooves

25 Complex Text Passages to Meet the Common Core: Literature and Informational Texts, Grade 2 © 2014 by Scholastic Teaching Resources

Name _____ Date _____

Unicorn Secrets

▶ **Answer each question. Give evidence from the fantasy.**

1 What do most people believe about unicorns?

○ A. Unicorns breathe fire.   ○ C. Unicorns are not real.

○ B. Unicorns are friendly.   ○ D. Unicorns are very smart.

What helped you pick your answer? _____

_____

2 What is the unicorn's secret for knowing if someone is telling the truth?

○ A. Swim every night in fresh cold water.

○ B. Sip goat's milk and dewdrops.

○ C. Talk to friends in the woods.

○ D. Look deeply into his or her eyes.

How did you pick your answer? _____

_____

3 In lines 7 and 8, the unicorn tells how to keep your *coat* clean.
What does the unicorn mean by *coat*?

_____

4 Which of the secrets make sense for people to follow? Explain.

_____

_____

_____

Name _____   Date _____

Chinese Calendar

What do the animals stand for in the Chinese calendar?

The Chinese calendar has 12 animal signs. Each animal stands for different ideas.

1 I am **Rat**. Polite, smart, steady, and careful, I stand for joy.

2 I am **Ox**. Patient, honest, calm, and good, I like all routines.

3 I am **Tiger**. Restless, brave, caring, and kind, I bring good luck.

4 I am **Rabbit**. Loving, honest, artistic, and lucky, I stand for quiet.

5 I am **Dragon**. Strong, active, important, and smart, I always stay positive.

6 I am **Snake**. Strong-minded, wise, deep, and proud, I look for beauty.

7 I am **Horse**. Well-liked, pleasing, chatty, and skilled, I enjoy outside sports.

8 I am **Sheep**. Artistic, neat, gentle, and shy, I bring true love.

9 I am **Monkey**. Pleasant, brainy, clever, and well-off, I seek all facts.

10 I am **Rooster**. Proud, cool, hard-working, and curious, I stand for order.

11 I am **Dog**. Trusty, honest, fair, and helpful, I believe in honor.

12 I am **Pig**. Polite, just, brave, and joyful, I have many friends.

Name _____ Date _____

Chinese Calendar

▶ **Answer each question. Give evidence from the article.**

1 Which animal in the Chinese calendar is friendly?

　○ A. Rat 　　○ B. Rabbit 　　○ C. Monkey 　　○ D. Pig

What helped you pick your answer? _____

_____

2 What do Rabbit and Sheep have in common?

　○ A. Both are honest. 　　○ C. Both are artistic.

　○ B. Both are gentle. 　　○ D. Both are strong.

How did you pick your answer? _____

_____

3 What is something good about Tiger (section 3)? _____

_____

What might be a problem for Tiger? _____

_____

4 Who is someone you know who could have been born in the Year
of the Monkey. Explain why.

_____

_____

_____

Name _____ Date _____

Word Wizard

What can you do when you read a word that has many meanings?

1   Suppose you are reading an interesting story.

2   Suddenly, you come to a word. You can read the word,

3   but the meanings you know for it just don't make sense.

4   Her albums were a **mine** of family history.

5   Lucky for you, there is a special book to help you. It is a

6   *dictionary*.

7   A dictionary gives a meaning for every word it lists.

8   Look up the word *mine*. Find the meaning that works

9   best in the sentence.

Entry word

How to say the word

10   **mine** (mine)

11   **1.** PRONOUN the one that belongs to me:

12   *This desk is mine.*

13   **2.** NOUN a large tunnel or space made in

14   the earth to dig out valuable things

15   **3.** NOUN a small bomb hidden underground

16   or underwater

Definitions
with part
of speech

17   **4.** VERB to dig minerals out of the ground:

18   *They mine silver down there.*

19   **5.** NOUN a rich supply:

20   *Dad is a mine of sports facts.*

Name _____ Date _____

Word Wizard

▶ **Answer each question. Give evidence from the passage.**

1 How many different meanings of *mine* does this dictionary entry give?

○ A. one   ○ B. three   ○ C. five   ○ D. seven

What helped you pick your answer? _____

_____

2 What does this dictionary entry NOT give?

○ A. other words that mean the same as *mine*

○ B. examples of sentences with *mine* in them

○ C. how to pronounce *mine*

○ D. how to spell *mine*

How did you pick your answer? _____

_____

3 Which meaning of *mine* fits the sentence in line 4? Explain. _____

_____

_____

4 Read this sentence: We visited an old copper *mine*.
Which meaning of *mine* best fits this sentence? Explain. _____

_____

_____

Name _____ Date _____

Old Superstition, Long Word

What is a superstition?

1   Good morning. Today I will
2 tell you something not to worry
3 about. I don't get how a number
4 could be scary. But poor 13
5 always gets picked on!
6   Do you fear the number 13?
7 If so, your problem comes from a
8 *superstition*. A superstition isn't a
9 fact, no matter how many people
10 think it is. My Aunt Marge is afraid of black cats. That
11 superstition keeps her from petting my cat Coal, who is as
12 sweet as pie. My brother Theo won't step on a crack. He
13 says it will "break our mother's back." That's just a silly
14 saying. It is totally untrue.
15   My mom is a math teacher. She taught me a long
16 hard word—*triskaidekaphobia*. [Hold up the sign.] You read
17 its chunks while I say them: TRISKAI…DEKA…PHOBIA.
18 Now say the whole word with me: tris-kai-de-ka-PHO-bi-a.
19   Good! This means fear of the number 13. Mom says
20 that the fear came after many bad things happened on a
21 Friday the 13th long ago. People couldn't explain why the
22 bad things happened so they blamed a number!
23   Well, I'm not afraid of 13. I can't wait to be 13 because
24 then I'll be a teenager. I was born on March 13, and I'm
25 not scary! I say NO more triskaidekaphobia! Thank you.

Name _____ Date _____

Old Superstition, Long Word

▶ **Answer each question. Give evidence from the speech.**

1 Which word means the same as *untrue* (line 14)?

○ A. silly   ○ B. false   ○ C. scary   ○ D. unfair

What helped you pick your answer? _____

_____

2 Which of the following sayings is a superstition?

○ A. Wearing socks keeps your feet warm.

○ B. Use an umbrella to stay dry in the rain.

○ C. Eating junk food is bad for your health.

○ D. Break a mirror and get seven years of bad luck.

How did you pick your answer? _____

_____

_____

3 Tell in your own words what a *superstition* is. _____

_____

_____

4 Why does the speaker talk about Aunt Marge and Theo? _____

_____

_____

Name _____ Date _____

Ask the Driver

How is an interview organized?

1   Rico rides the school bus.
2   He is the first one picked up each
3   day. He is the last one dropped
4   off after school. When he had to
5   ask an adult questions about the
6   job they do, Rico asked Wanda.
7   She is his bus driver.

8   **Rico:** *Wanda, how did you become a bus driver?*
9   **Wanda:** I like kids and driving, so I took bus driving lessons.
10   Once I passed my driver tests, I looked for work at different
11   schools.

12   **Rico:** *Were you scared at first?*
13   **Wanda:** No, but I worry about keeping you kids safe. We get
14   bad weather sometimes. Or I might feel sick now and then.
15   But I have a perfect safety record. I'm proud of that.

16   **Rico:** *When do you have to get up?*
17   **Wanda:** I wake up at 5:30 A.M. I have tea and toast, and
18   then drive my car to the bus garage. I check my bus and fill it
19   with gas. I leave by 7:00 A.M. to reach my first stop on time.

20   **Rico:** *Why don't you play music on the bus?*
21   **Wanda:** I don't want any extra sounds. I need to pay
22   attention and listen for kids who may call for help.

Name _____ Date _____

Ask the Driver

▶ **Answer each question. Give evidence from the interview.**

1 How does Rico know Wanda?

○ A. Wanda drives the school bus Rico rides.

○ C. Rico lives next door to Wanda.

○ B. Wanda is Rico's music teacher.

○ D. Rico is her son.

What helped you pick your answer? _____

_____

2 What does it mean that Wanda has a *perfect safety record* (line 15)?

○ A. She did very well on her bus driver test.

○ B. She has never had an accident driving her bus.

○ C. She knows all about how to give first aid.

○ D. She always picks up her riders on time.

How did you pick your answer? _____

_____

3 Why might Rico have had to ask questions about an adult's job (lines 4–6)?

_____

4 Write two other questions to ask a school bus driver about the job.

_____

_____

_____

Name _____ Date _____

The ABCs of 9-1-1

How does this poster present information?

9-1-1

1 **What is 9-1-1?**
2   9-1-1 is a FREE phone
3   number to call in an
4   emergency. Call 9-1-1 for
5   FAST help for yourself or
6   someone else.

7 **When do I call 9-1-1?**
8   Dial 9-1-1 ONLY if a
9   person is hurt or in
10 danger. Dial for help
11 from the police, a doctor,
12 or a firefighter.

13 **Who answers?**
14 The person who answers
15 knows how to get you the
16 right kind of help. That
17 person will ask questions.
18 Your answers guide the
19 9-1-1 operator to the help
20 you need most.

21 **Why must I answer**
22 **questions?**
23 The operator must know
24 who you are, where you
25 are, and what's wrong.
26 He or she will also tell
27 you what to do until help
28 gets there.

29 **How do I talk to the**
30 **operator?**
31 Stay calm. Speak clearly.
32 Describe the problem with
33 facts, such as your exact
34 address and full name.

35 **When is the call over?**
36 Stay on until you get the
37 OK to hang up. Even if
38 you have nothing more to
39 say, let the operator hear
40 what's going on.

Name _____ Date _____

The ABCs of 9-1-1

▶ **Answer each question. Give evidence from the poster.**

1 Which would also make a good title for this poster?

○ A. How to Make a Telephone Call   ○ C. When You Have a Bad Cold

○ B. What to Do in an Emergency   ○ D. Who Invented 9-1-1?

What helped you pick your answer? _____

_____

_____

2 Which is not an *emergency*?

○ A. A fire breaks out in the kitchen.

○ B. A person falls and is too hurt to get up.

○ C. There is a squirrel in the attic.

○ D. A worker gets badly cut by a saw.

How did you pick your answer? _____

_____

3 When does a 9-1-1 call end? _____

_____

4 Why is it important to stay calm and speak clearly when you call 9-1-1?

_____

_____

Name _____ Date _____

A Hidden Message

Why is it important to follow the directions?

1   It's fun and easy to make **invisible paint**. It uses
2 normal materials most people already have. Gather up
3 everything you need. Then follow the steps to surprise
4 your friends.

5 **What You Need**
6 • tablespoon measure
7 • baking soda
8 • paper cup
9 • water
10 • mixing stick
11 • paintbrush
12 • plain white paper

13 **What You Do**
14 **1.** Measure 3 tablespoons of baking soda into
15   the paper cup.
16 **2.** Add 4 tablespoons of water to the cup.
17   Mix until all lumps are gone.
18 **3.** Dip a paintbrush into the "paint."
19   Write a message on the paper.
20 **4.** Let the paint dry until your message disappears!
21 **5.** Hold the paper in front of a lit lightbulb.
22   The heat will turn the baking soda brown.
23   Your message will reappear!

Name _____ Date _____

A Hidden Message

▶ **Answer each question. Give evidence from the instructions.**

1 Which word in the first paragraph means "cannot be seen"?

○ A. easy   ○ B. normal   ○ C. surprise   ○ D. invisible

What helped you pick your answer? _____

_____

2 What will *surprise your friends* (lines 3 and 4)?

○ A. An invisible message reappears.

○ B. Most of the materials are easy to find.

○ C. You can paint with baking soda.

○ D. Mixing makes lumps go away.

How did you pick your answer? _____

_____

_____

3 What do you do after you write a message on the paper (lines 18 and 19)?

_____

_____

4 Why are the **What You Do** steps numbered (lines 13–23)? _____

_____

_____

Name _____ Date _____

It's About Time

In what ways is information presented?

1   People spend lots of time thinking about time. *When do we*
2 *go to art class? How much time until recess? How long does the*
3 *movie last?*
4   Time is a large but hidden idea. You can't see, hear, touch,
5 taste, or smell time. But you notice hints that time passes.
6 A few hours after lunch you may feel your tummy rumble
7 with hunger. You know that time passes after swimming
8 because your hair changes from wet to dry.
9   Helpful words let us compare when things happen. We
10 learn words like *before, now,* and *later.* An old saying helps
11 children remember three major time words:

12   **Yesterday** was past,
13   **today** won't last, and
14   **tomorrow** comes fast.

15   This table shows time facts.
16 Which do you know by heart?

1 minute	=	60 seconds
1 hour	=	60 minutes
1 day	=	24 hours
1 week	=	7 days
1 month	=	28 to 31 days

Sand clocks show time passing.

Name _____ Date _____

It's About Time

▶ **Answer each question. Give evidence from the article.**

1 Why does the writer ask questions in lines 1–3?

○ A. The writer needs to know some answers.

○ B. The writer wants readers to give answers.

○ C. The writer gives examples of how people think.

○ D. The writer doesn't know when you will read this.

What helped you pick your answer? _____

_____

_____

2 Use the table. Which measure of time has 60 minutes?

○ A. 1 day   ○ B. 1 hour   ○ C. 1 minute   ○ D. 1 month

How did you pick your answer? _____

_____

3 Explain what the writer means by saying that time is a *hidden idea* (line 4).

_____

_____

4 Look at the sand clocks. How do they show that time passes? _____

_____

_____

Name _____ Date _____

About an Illustrator

Why does the writer use Pinkney's own words?

1 Jerry Pinkney is a "storyteller
2 at heart." He has been a book
3 illustrator for nearly 50 years.
4 He has made the art for more
5 than 100 books. Many of them
6 have won awards.

7 Pinkney began drawing as
8 a young boy. He says, "At some
9 point I realized I'd rather sit and
10 draw than do almost anything
11 else." By first grade, he was the
12 class artist. He always had a pad
13 and pencil with him. When he
14 wasn't using them, he would
15 look for little details all around him.

Jerry Pinkney

16 But school wasn't easy for Pinkney. He didn't read
17 as well as other kids did. No matter how hard he tried,
18 he was a slow reader. He recalls, "I felt calm when I was
19 making pictures. When I was drawing, I knew that I was
20 using my mind."

21 Pinkney focuses hard when he draws. "I don't see
22 things until I draw them. When I put a line down, the
23 only thing I know is how it should feel. I know when it
24 doesn't feel right. I work with a pencil in one hand and
25 an eraser in the other." He believes that every mistake is
26 a new chance to do better.

Name _____ Date _____

About an Illustrator

▶ **Answer each question. Give evidence from the passage.**

1 Jerry Pinkney knew that he was using his mind when he was _____.

○ A. in first grade   ○ C. making pictures

○ B. trying to read   ○ D. carrying a pad and pencil

What helped you pick your answer? _____

_____

2 What job do illustrators do?

○ A. Illustrators erase things.   ○ C. Illustrators write books.

○ B. Illustrators win awards.   ○ D. Illustrators make pictures.

How did you pick your answer? _____

_____

_____

3 Explain why school was hard for young Jerry Pinkney. _____

_____

_____

4 Why doesn't Jerry Pinkney worry about making mistakes when he draws?
Explain.

_____

_____

_____

Name _____ Date _____

Making Coins

How do pictures help explain the text?

1   A mint is a candy with a fresh, tingly flavor. But did
2   you know that there is another kind of mint, too? A mint
3   is also the place where coins are made. Every American
4   coin is made at one of four U. S. mints.
5   There are many steps to making a coin. Here are the
6   main parts.

7   (1) A big machine punches disks from thin
8   sheets of metal. These disks are called
9   *blanks*. They have no designs yet.

10 (2) The blanks get heated, washed, and dried.
11 Then they go through another machine
12 that raises a rim around the edge.

13 (3) Now the blanks go to the *coining press*. It
14 stamps each blank with the designs for
15 both sides. This is called *striking*.

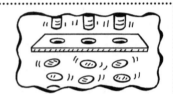

16 (4) Workers closely check the coins to be sure
17 they look right. Coins with mistakes get
18 sent back to be recycled.

19 (5) A special machine counts the coins. Then it
20 pours them into huge bags. Forklift trucks
21 move the bags into giant safes.

22 (6) The last stop is the bank. Then the new
23 coins can get to the people who will
24 spend them!

Name _____ Date _____

Making Coins

▶ **Answer each question. Give evidence from the text.**

1 What is the job of the coining press?

○ A. It puts the designs on both sides of the coin.

○ B. It decides which designs a coin gets.

○ C. It punches out disks from thin metal.

○ D. It sends the coins out to the banks.

What helped you pick your answer? _____

_____

2 What happens after *striking* (line 15)?

○ A. The disks get punched.   ○ C. The coins get washed and dried.

○ B. The coins arrive at   ○ D. Workers check the coins
    the bank.   for mistakes.

How did you pick your answer? _____

_____

3 Reread lines 7–9. Why are the metal disks called *blanks*? _____

_____

_____

4 Why are the bags of coins put into giant safes? How do you know?

_____

_____

Name _____ Date _____

Horse Sense

How does the title fit the essay?

1 Sayings can stand for something other than what
2 the words seem to mean. Such sayings are called
3 *idioms.* Suppose your dad says, "Hold your tongue!"
4 Does he want you to grab your tongue? No, he wants
5 you to stop talking.

6 English has many *horse* idioms. This may be
7 because so many people used to have or use horses.
8 Teachers might ask groups to *stop horsing around.* This
9 means to stop acting wild and noisy.

10 Did you ever get a bad leg cramp? A nurse might
11 call it a *Charley horse,* no matter what your name is!
12 Nobody knows for sure how this old idiom got started.

13 Can you trust a report that *comes straight from the*
14 *horse's mouth?* Usually you can. This idiom means
15 that the person who reported the event was there
16 when it happened.

17 *Don't put the cart*
18 *before the horse* is a
19 warning: Do things in
20 order. If you zip your
21 jacket before you put
22 it on, you put the cart
23 before the horse. Maybe
24 you do this because you
25 have no *horse sense*!

25 Complex Text Passages to Meet the Common Core: Literature and Informational Texts, Grade 2 © 2014 by Scholastic Teaching Resources

Name _____ Date _____

Horse Sense

▶ **Answer each question. Give evidence from the essay.**

1 Which of the following is NOT an idiom?

○ A. Comes straight from the horse's mouth   ○ C. Stop horsing around!

○ B. Feed hay to that hungry horse!   ○ D. Hold your tongue!

What helped you pick your answer? _____

_____

_____

2 Which shows *Don't put the cart before the horse*?

○ A. eating your cereal and then pouring milk in the bowl

○ B. opening the closet and then hanging up your coat

○ C. putting on your socks and then your shoes

○ D. washing the dishes and then drying them

How did you pick your answer? _____

_____

3 Explain what an idiom is. _____

_____

_____

4 What does it mean to have *horse sense* (title and line 25)? Explain.

_____

_____

Name _____ Date _____

Bikes: Yes or No?

How does the writer organize the details?

1 **The Question** Should second graders ride bikes to
2 school? Most kids love the idea, but many adults do
3 not. There are good and bad reasons for it. Think about
4 these points.

5 **Yes!** Most kids love riding their bikes. It feels grown-
6 up to get around on our own. Riding a bike is good
7 exercise. It makes kids practice being safe and
8 responsible. If more kids rode to school, our roads would
9 have fewer buses and cars on them. That would bring
10 cleaner air and fewer traffic jams.

11 **No!** Adults worry that second graders are too young to
12 ride to school. Some would get lost. Others would not
13 obey the safety rules. It would be hard to carry books,
14 projects, and lunches. It would be risky to ride in rain
15 or snow. And what about kids who don't have bikes or
16 who cannot ride?

17 **My Plan** I want to bike to
18 school, but we need some
19 changes first. Let's ask the town
20 to build safe bike lanes. Let's
21 get kids to promise to wear
22 helmets. Let's say that all bikes
23 need baskets or saddle packs.

Name _____ Date _____

Bikes: Yes or No?

▶ **Answer each question. Give evidence from the essay.**

1 Which is a reason the writer gives for letting kids ride bikes to school?

○ A. Kids would get to school faster. ○ C. There are bike lanes for kids.

○ B. Riding a bike is good exercise. ○ D. Some kids would get lost.

What helped you pick your answer? _____

_____

_____

2 Which is NOT something a responsible bike rider would do?

○ A. Wear a helmet. ○ C. Ride fast through stop signs.

○ B. Stay in a bike lane. ○ D. Use a bike basket.

How did you pick your answer? _____

_____

_____

3 Describe how the **bolded** words help you follow the writer's ideas.

_____

_____

4 Who wrote this essay? How can you tell? _____

_____

_____

Name _____ Date _____

Good Citizens

What is a good citizen?

1   How can second graders be good citizens? This isn't a
2 hard question. You already do many of the right things if
3 you act with kindness and common sense.
4   A *citizen* has the **right** to belong to a group. In turn, that
5 citizen promises to take part in that group. This is a citizen's
6 **responsibility**. You began life as a brand new citizen of the
7 world on the day you were born. Your caregivers were your
8 very first group. Your main right was to be cared for. Your
9 first responsibility was to grow and learn.
10   Now that you are older, you are a citizen of other groups
11 where you live. You are a citizen of your neighborhood, your
12 school, your city, and your country. As a good citizen, you do
13 the best you can to help your many communities.
14   Here are five steps any good citizen can follow:

15   **1.** Care, share, and treat yourself
16   and others with respect.
17   **2.** Cooperate and try your best to
18   be honest, fair, and kind.
19   **3.** Do your part to live, work, and
20   play by the rules.
21   **4.** Make the best choices you can
22   about right and wrong.
23   **5.** Be a good neighbor that others
24   know they can count on.

Name _____ Date _____

Good Citizens

▶ **Answer each question. Give evidence from the essay.**

1 When do people start being citizens?

  ○ A. when they are born   ○ C. when they start going to school

  ○ B. when they learn to walk   ○ D. when they vote for the first time

How can you prove your answer? _____

_____

2 Which is NOT something good citizens do?

  ○ A. Clean up after a picnic in the park.

  ○ B. Obey the leash law when they walk a dog.

  ○ C. Help young children cross the street safely.

  ○ D. Pick a neighbor's flowers without asking first.

What helped you pick your answer? _____

_____

3 What does it mean to *count on* someone (line 24)? _____

_____

_____

4 Look closely at the picture. Tell why it belongs with an essay on good citizens.

_____

_____

Name _____ Date _____

The String Family

Why do some instruments make a family?

1 Instruments belong to families. They don't really have
2 mothers and fathers. But instruments in the same family are
3 related, just like people are.

4 Most string instruments have bodies that are made of
5 wood. All instruments in the *string family* make sound in the
6 same way. Each one has strings that are stretched tightly on
7 it. The strings can be made of metal, nylon, or strong animal
8 fibers called *gut*.

9 String instruments cannot make sound on their own. They
10 must have someone who can play them. The player must
11 touch one or more strings to make them *vibrate*. To vibrate
12 means to move back and forth very fast. It is the vibrating
13 that makes the sounds you hear.

14 The chart shows two ways players can make strings move.

BOW	PLUCK
Players rub a **bow** across the strings. A bow is a thin wooden tool. It has long horsehairs from end to end. 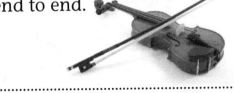	Players **pluck** at strings with fingers or fingernails. Or they can use a small plastic tool called a **pick**. 
Bow: fiddle, violin, viola, cello, double bass	***Pluck:*** guitar, banjo, harp, ukulele

25 Complex Text Passages to Meet the Common Core: Literature and Informational Texts, Grade 2 © 2014 by Scholastic Teaching Resources

Name _____ Date _____

The String Family

▶ **Answer each question. Give evidence from the essay.**

1 How do ALL string instruments make sound?

○ A. They have strings made of metal.   ○ C. They have wooden bodies.

○ B. They have strings that vibrate.   ○ D. They are plucked.

What helped you pick your answer? _____

_____

_____

2 Which is a tool players use to make a string instrument vibrate?

○ A. a gut   ○ B. a pluck   ○ C. a pick   ○ D. a string

How did you pick your answer? _____

_____

3 Explain why a drum does NOT belong to the string family. _____

_____

_____

4 Why would the author use the word *family* to describe things that are not people? Explain.

_____

_____

Name _____ Date _____

Changes in Rocks

How are *erosion* and *weathering* related?

1 Most rocks are so hard you may think they can't
2 break. But many forces break down rocks. It doesn't take a
3 hammer or machine. Nature itself can change rocks.
4   *Erosion* is the word scientists use for when things wear
5 away. When big rocks *erode*, little bits of them break off.
6 Erosion makes rocks change their size and shape. Weather
7 causes some kinds of erosion. This kind of erosion is called
8 *weathering*. Changes from weathering take a long time.

9 **Weathering by Water** When it rains,
10 water gets into cracks in rocks. If the weather
11 gets very cold, the water can freeze. Frozen
12 water takes up more space than liquid water.
13 So ice in a rock can make it crack or break.

14 **Weathering by Wind** Blowing winds can
15 carry dust and pebbles that hit against big
16 rocks. Bit by bit, all that rubbing erodes the
17 rock. So weathering by wind causes changes
18 in size and shape.

19 **Weathering by Waves** Ocean waves are
20 strong. They move toward the land and crash
21 into rocks at the shore. As waves hit the rocks
22 again and again, little bits chip off. In time,
23 many of those little chips turn into sand.

Name _____ Date _____

Changes in Rocks

▶ **Answer each question. Give evidence from the article.**

1 What does *erosion* do to big rocks?

○ A. It gets them wet.   ○ C. It breaks them down.

○ B. It builds them up.   ○ D. It makes them heavier.

What helped you pick your answer? _____

_____

2 Which sentence about weathering is TRUE?

○ A. Weathering happens very quickly.

○ B. Weathering must take place near water.

○ C. Weathering works only on broken rock.

○ D. Weathering takes place over a long time.

How did you pick your answer? _____

_____

3 Explain how wind erodes big rocks. _____

_____

_____

4 Describe the kind of weathering that changed the rock in each picture.

_____

_____

_____

Name _____ Date _____

A Sweet Museum

Who might read a museum review?

1   Vermont is a small state with many mountains. In those
2 mountains grow many maple trees. So it makes sense that
3 Vermont has a maple museum.

4   **Making Maple Syrup** The New England Maple Museum is
5 small and plain outside but inside, visitors go back in time. They
6 learn all about maple syrup. They see old photos of sap buckets
7 hanging from maple trees. Murals painted around the walls
8 show the sap being boiled. There are old tools and handmade
9 buckets. Children can even make maple candy and taste it, too!

10   **The Legend** Many visitors say that the best thing about the
11 maple museum is a legend they learn about. It says that maple
12 syrup came from a happy accident. An Indian hunter dropped
13 his things under a maple tree. He pounded his axe into the trunk
14 for safety. The next day, he removed his axe.
15 Watery sap dripped down into his wooden
16 bowl. The sap had no taste. But then it was
17 boiled over a wood fire. It turned brown and
18 thick and sweet!

19   **Syrup Today** Today people still make
20 maple syrup the same way. They use gas
21 stoves instead of wood fires, but the sweet
22 taste is the same. Discover the sweetness for
23 yourself. The Maple Museum is worth a visit!

Name _____ Date _____

A Sweet Museum

▶ **Answer each question. Give evidence from the review.**

1 What made watery sap turn brown, thick, and sweet?

○ A. an axe   ○ C. a wooden bowl

○ B. an old tool   ○ D. the heat of a fire

What helped you pick your answer? _____

_____

_____

2 Which best describes *murals* (line 7)?

○ A. modern photos   ○ C. stacks of old sap buckets

○ B. pictures painted on walls   ○ D. sweet things made of maple syrup

How did you pick your answer? _____

_____

_____

3 Why does the maple syrup bottle have that shape? _____

_____

4 What makes this article a review? Explain. _____

_____

_____

_____

Name _____ Date _____

Who Wrote What?

How can you tell who wrote which part of the postcard?

1 Hi Dad,
2   So far our trip has been way fun!
3 Last night, we camped near a place
4 called Heart Lake. Elsa thinks it
5 might be named because it has the
6 shape of a heart. But we can't tell.
7 Too bad we don't have a helicopter so
8 we could fly over it and look down!
9   We set up our tent on a little hill for a good
10 view. We made a campfire inside a ring of stones
11 we gathered. We all ate hot dogs on buns,
12 beans, and toasted marshmallows, of course!
13 But I'm tired of the same food every night.
14 Oh, for some of your best mac and cheese!
15   This morning, Mom let us take a swim before
16 we packed. It's cloudy now, so I'm glad we got
17 to swim a little. The only bad part was all the
18 bug bites we got. Mom calls us the McScratch
19 family.
20   *We miss you like crazy, but we'll be home next*
21 *week. Give Ruffles lots of ear scratches from us.*
22 *And don't forget to go shopping. Please stock up*
23 *on fresh fruit and veggies! Too bad the kids are*
24 *still too young to drive!*
25   *Hugs and kisses, Greg, Elsa & Mom*

From:
The McScratch Family
Near Heart Lake
Somewhere, USA

To:
Mr. Nelson McNeill
518 Locust Drive
Endwell, NM 74629

25 Complex Text Passages to Meet the Common Core: Literature and Informational Texts, Grade 2 © 2014 by Scholastic Teaching Resources

Name _____ Date _____

Who Wrote What?

▶ **Answer each question. Give evidence from the postcard.**

1 When you *stock up* on something (line 22), you _____.

  ○ A. cook some of it   ○ C. put it in a box

  ○ B. get a lot of it   ○ D. feed it to your cattle

  What helped you pick your answer? _____

  _____

  _____

2 Which family member complains about bugs?

  ○ A. Elsa   ○ B. Greg   ○ C. Mom   ○ D. Ruffles

  How did you pick your answer? _____

  _____

  _____

3 Who is Nelson McNeill? What clues tell you? _____

  _____

  _____

4 Who wrote the last paragraph? What clues tell you? _____

  _____

  _____

  _____

Literature Passages

Passage 1: Raining Frogs?

1. B; Sample answer: The story says Goran was in bed with the flu, so he was sick (lines 2–3). **2.** D; Sample answer: The story says that winds can spin very fast, like a tornado. So, I picked the word most like *spins* (lines 18–19). **3.** Sample answer: Mama was testing how warm he felt to see if he had a fever. **4.** Sample answer: A mystery has something you don't know but have to figure out. This story is about the mystery of raining frogs (lines 18–22).

Passage 2: Sit, Stay, Read

1. D; Sample answer: Wrigley comes in with his owner, so that must be who Mr. Lim is (lines 8–11). **2.** C; Sample answer: The author says that Zuri never worries when she reads to Wrigley because he is so patient (lines 21–22). **3.** Sample answer: Zuri treats Wrigley like any other listener and helps him understand how the pictures go with the words of the story (lines 19–20). **4.** Sample answer: A cozy corner would be small, quiet, have pillows or a rug, and good light for reading. It would be away from other kids.

Passage 3: The Stonecutter

1. B; Sample answer: I reread the beginning and saw that Tasaku first asked to become a prince (lines 3–6). **2.** C; Sample answer: Tasaku was never kind or loving (lines 15–16, lines 19–20), but always wanted more (lines 20–21). No matter what he became or got, it never really made him happy, so we should learn to be happy with what we have (line 24). **3.** Sample answer: When you envy somebody, you want or long for what that person has. **4.** Sample answer: I think Tasaku will beg to be a stonecutter again. When he was a stonecutter he had a good life (lines 1–3), but then he got too greedy.

Passage 4: Breaker Boy

1. B; Sample answer: The author says that the breaker room was as hot as an oven (lines 6–7).

2. A; Sample answer: His family needed money (lines 18–20), so he had to make the boss think he was old enough (lines 1–3). **3.** Sample answer: A breaker boy takes out everything that isn't coal (lines 9–12). **4.** Sample answer: Boys are sitting on wooden benches. They are picking through coal (lines 6, 9–12) while bent over (15–17).

Passage 5: Wenebojo Gets Angry

1. A; Sample answer: It says in lines 1 and 2 what Wenebojo did. **2.** D; Sample answer: Fox's job was to warn small animals like the little birds, but he didn't do it, so their nests got trampled (lines 4–7). **3.** Sample answer: It shows the hump on Buffalo's back and his head hanging low (lines 16–18) and Fox in a hole in the ground (lines 20–21). **4.** Sample answer: Buffalo hung his head and humped his shoulders. This means he knew he was wrong (line 12).

Passage 6: Crows in the Corn

1. A; Sample answer: She did everything in B, C, and D, but those weren't the odd things. It was odd that she slept late (lines 1–2). **2.** C; Sample answer: I read that the crows flew to the field of corn to feast. So ripe corn must be ready to eat since they liked it so much (lines 4–5). **3.** Sample answer: The farmer didn't get up to chase them away, so they kept eating until all the corn was gone (lines 2–5, 7–12). **4.** Sample answer: If you say it out loud, it sounds like the word *corn* and like "caw," which crows say. I think it's a little joke.

Passage 7: The Golden Touch

1. B; Sample answer: Midas cried, "NO MORE!" because his daughter turned into a statue. He couldn't take it anymore and was sad (lines 19–22). **2.** A; Sample answer: In line 7, I read that he loved his new power. So, I think *giddy* means *joyful*. **3.** Sample answer: He was already the richest person on Earth (lines 1–3). Plus, everything turned to gold, so there was nothing to eat or drink (lines 13–17). **4.** Sample answer: He went to bed hungry the night before (lines 16–17), and he was really happy his daughter was okay again (lines 24–25).

Passage 8: The Napping Dog

1. D; Sample answer: The story says that the dog came back over and over and did the same thing each time (lines 11–13). Brushing their teeth is something kids do every day. **2.** C; Sample answer: It can't be A or B. The note says that Scooter's family has a lot of young kids, and Scooter needs some rest. The last sentence sounds like something a mom or dad would say. So, I think one of them is the owner and wrote the note. **3.** Sample answer: The dog wears a collar and has tags (lines 2–4). **4.** Sample answer: The note on his collar says that he lives in a family with five young kids. With all those kids, it might be busy and noisy there. So, maybe he just wants to find a quiet place (lines 21–24).

Passage 9: Unicorn Secrets

1. C; Sample answer: It says in lines 1 and 2 that most people say that unicorns aren't real, so that's why I picked C. **2.** D; Sample answer: The unicorn said A and B (lines 7 and 9), but those aren't about telling the truth. So, I picked D, which is about truth (lines 15–16). **3.** Sample answer: I think it means the hair on the outside of the body. In the picture, the unicorn has a mane and a tail and looks like a horse. And a horse's body is covered with hair. **4.** Sample answer: Except for eating cobwebs, each secret has some good ideas in it. It's good to be clean (lines 7–8), to drink milk (lines 9–10), to exercise (lines 13–14), to look into people's eyes when they speak (lines 15–16), and to pick your friends carefully (lines 17–19).

> **Informational Text Passages**

Passage 10: Chinese Calendar

Note: In this passage, each section of captioned text is numbered, rather than individual lines of text.

1. D; Sample answer: I read that Pig has many friends (section 12). **2.** C; Sample answer: I read about Rabbit (section 4) and Sheep (section 8), and looked for the same word describing both of them. **3.** Sample answer: One good thing about Tiger is

that he is brave, but he is also restless. That might make someone get bored easily and get into trouble (section 3). **4.** Sample answer: (Answers will vary, but should refer to a person who is pleasant, brainy, clever, or is not poor.) For example: My friend Doug is very smart. He likes to read a lot and solve puzzles. That sounds like how a person born in the year of the Monkey would be (section 9).

Passage 11: Word Wizard

1. C; Sample answer: I counted the number of different meanings. There are five (line 19). **2.** A; Sample answer: I read all the choices. Only A wasn't there (lines 10–20). **3.** Sample answer: I think it is meaning 5. In that meaning and in the sentence, *mine* is used in the same way (lines 19–20). **4.** Sample answer: I think it is meaning 2—a large tunnel or space made in the earth to dig out valuable things. Copper is something they dug out of that old mine (lines 13–14).

Passage 12: Old Superstition, Long Word

1. B; Sample answer: In lines 8 and 9, it says that a superstition isn't a fact. So, it is not true. *False* means *not true*. **2.** D; Sample answer: The first three are true and make sense. D sounds silly and untrue. **3.** Sample answer: A superstition is something people believe in that isn't really true (lines 8–10, 12–14, 21–22). **4.** Sample answer: Aunt Marge and Theo both believe in superstitions. The person reading the speech tells about them to show how silly superstitions can be (lines 10–14).

Passage 13: Ask the Driver

1. A; Sample answer: It says in lines 6 and 7 that Wanda is Rico's bus driver. **2.** B; Sample answer: A, C, and D might be true, but they aren't about safety. **3.** Sample answer: Maybe his class is learning about jobs and it was his homework, or maybe his class was learning how to do interviews. **4.** Sample answers: What is the best part of your job? What do you do between the morning and afternoon routes? What did you learn in bus driving class?

Passage 14: The ABCs of 9-1-1

1. B; Sample answer: I know that this poster is about what to do in an emergency, so B is a good answer. The other choices don't fit. **2.** C; Sample answer: An emergency is something very serious. In lines 8–10, it says to call 9-1-1 only if someone is hurt or in danger. Fire, bad falls, and deep cuts are emergencies. A squirrel in an attic is not. **3.** Sample answer: It ends when the operator says it's OK to hang up (lines 36–37). **4.** Sample answer: The 9-1-1 operator will ask questions to find out details about what's wrong (lines 16–20, 23–28). So, if you stay calm and speak clearly, you can say the important stuff (lines 31–34) and get the right help as soon as possible.

Passage 15: A Hidden Message

1. D; Sample answer: In line 20, it says that the message will disappear. If something disappears, you can't see it. **2.** A; Sample answer: The message you paint disappears, and then shows up again in brown (lines 22–23). B, C, and D are true but are not surprising. **3.** Sample answer: You let the paint dry until the message disappears (line 20). **4.** Sample answer: You have to do them in a certain order. The numbers tell you that.

Passage 16: It's About Time

1. C; Sample answer: In the very first sentence, the writer says that people spend time thinking about time. So, I think the questions are examples of thoughts people have about time. **2.** B; Sample answer: I looked through the table to find where it shows 60 minutes. I looked across and saw that it equals 1 hour. **3.** Sample answer: You can't see, hear, touch, taste, or smell time (lines 4–5). **4.** Sample answer: The sand starts out in the top part. As time passes, the sand goes down through a little hole in the skinny part and falls into the bottom.

Passage 17: About an Illustrator

1. C; Sample answer: I read that Jerry Pinkney knew he was using his mind when he was drawing (lines 19–20). **2.** D; Sample answer: I read that Jerry Pinkney has been a book illustrator for almost 50 years, and he made the art for more than 100 books (lines 2–5). **3.** Sample answer: Jerry Pinkney didn't read as well as the other kids did, no matter how hard he tried (lines 16–18). **4.** Sample answer: He believes that mistakes are a new chance to do better, and he works with a pencil and an eraser all the time (lines 24–26).

Passage 18: Making Coins

1. A; Sample answer: I found step 3, which tells about the coining press. It says that it stamps each blank with designs (lines 13–15). **2.** D; Sample answer: I found where it said *striking* (line 15). Then I read what came next. In step 4, it says that workers check coins and coins with mistakes get sent back to be recycled (lines 16–18). **3.** Sample answer: They don't have any designs on them yet. They are blank on both sides (lines 7–9). **4.** Sample answer: I know that coins are a kind of money. In lines 19 and 20, it says that the coins go into huge bags. The picture in step 5 shows a lot of them going into a bag. So, each bag must be worth a lot of money! Putting the bags in safes makes sure no one can take the coins. And because the bags are huge, the safes have to be giant-sized!

Passage 19: Horse Sense

1. B; Sample answer: I found three of the four idioms in the essay (lines 3, 8, 13–14), so I picked the one that wasn't there. **2.** A; Sample answer: I read each choice and figured out which one was backward, or in the wrong order (lines 17–23). **3.** Sample answer: An idiom is a saying. The words in it can stand for something different than what you think they mean (lines 1–5). **4.** Sample answer: I think *horse sense* is like common sense because, of course, you zip your jacket after you put it on (lines 19–20).

Passage 20: Bikes: Yes or No?

1. B; Sample answer: I looked for reasons in the *Yes!* part of the essay, and found this reason (lines 6–7). **2.** C; Sample answer: *Safe* and *responsible* are listed together (lines 7–8), so I think that *responsible* means being careful to stay safe. Then I read all the choices, and C is not careful or safe. **3.** Sample answer: This essay has four parts. The bolded words in the first part tell that the writer will ask a question (lines 1–4). The next part gives some "yes" reasons (lines 5–10). The part after that gives "no" reasons (lines 11–16). It ends with the writer's own plan (lines 17–23). **4.** Sample answer: I think the writer is a kid. The writer wants to be able to bike to school, too, so the writer must be a kid (lines 17–23).

Passage 21: Good Citizens

1. A; Sample answer: In lines 6 and 7, it says that I began life as a brand new citizen of the world. **2.** D; Sample answer: I read the list of steps good citizens do. Then I read all four choices. D is not something a good neighbor does (lines 15–24). **3.** Sample answer: If you're a good neighbor that people can count on, you are probably someone who is honest, keeps promises, and helps when people need you. So, *count on* means someone who will be there for others (lines 17–20, 23–24). **4.** Sample answer: The tree is made of lots of different hands. It makes me think of many citizens working together to make a community strong and healthy, like a big tree.

Passage 22: The String Family

1. B; Sample answer: I reread lines 5 and 6. It says that all string instruments make sound the same way. Then I reread lines 10 and 11 to find out that strings vibrate to make sound. **2.** C; Sample answer: I looked at the right side of the chart. I saw that *pluck* is how you can move strings, but a *pick* is a tool. **3.** Sample answer: To play a drum, you bang on it. The sound a drum makes does not come from strings that vibrate. **4.** Sample answer: People in a family are related to each other because they belong together. Other things can be related, too. In science, I learned about the plant family and the insect family. So, I think the author uses *family* in that way.

Passage 23: Changes in Rocks

1. C; Sample answer: Erosion makes rocks change their size and shape by wearing them away and breaking off parts (lines 5–6). **2.** D; Sample answer:

In line 8, it says that changes from weathering take a long time. **3.** Sample answer: Wind blows little bits of dust and pebbles up against big rocks. This rubbing makes bits of the big rock break off (lines 14–18). **4.** Sample answer: Picture 1 shows a rock cracked by water (lines 9–13). It looks like a broken heart. Picture 2 shows rocks weathered by wind (lines 14–18). They look lumpy and rough, like they were scraped. Picture 3 shows weathering by waves, which wore away a big hole in the middle (lines 19–23).

Passage 24: A Sweet Museum

1. D; Sample answer: In the part about the legend, it says that the sap had no taste but then it was boiled over a wood fire (lines 16–18). **2.** B; Sample answer: It says there were murals painted around the walls. So, I think murals are pictures painted on walls (lines 7–8). **3.** Sample answer: I think it's shaped like a leaf because the sap used to make it came from a maple tree (lines 6–7). **4.** Sample answer: The writer says people should visit the museum (line 22–23) and gives reasons why. The writer tells about what visitors say they like best about the museum, and all the interesting things to see, learn, and do there (lines 4–18).

Passage 25: Who Wrote What?

1. B; Sample answer: At the end of the postcard, in line 22, it says, "don't forget to go shopping." You go shopping to buy things. So, I think it means get a lot of them, because the note says to be sure to get those things. **2.** A; Sample answer: I looked for the part where someone was complaining about bugs (lines 17–18). But I wasn't sure who it was yet. Then I reread the postcard. The writer of the first part talks about Elsa (lines 4–6), and the writer of the last part talks about the kids (lines 23–24). So, I figured out that Elsa wrote the part in the middle. **3.** Sample answer: He's the dad of Elsa and Greg and husband to their mom. I know because the postcard has his address on it and says, "Hi Dad" (line 1). **4.** Sample answer: Mom wrote the last paragraph because she reminds Dad what foods to buy (lines 22–23), and she talks about the kids (lines 23–24).

Notes

25 Complex Text Passages to Meet the Common Core: Literature and Informational Texts, Grade 2 © 2014 by Scholastic Teaching Resources